Let's Learn!
Engineering English
for Practical Applications

Shawn Andersson
Maho Nakahashi
Ryogo Yanagida

Osaka
University
Press

Introduction

As globalization progresses, the ability to collaborate in English with researchers from different backgrounds and transmit results to the world has become vital. However, many students in engineering and science majors lack confidence in their English communication capability. This textbook focuses on improving important and practical English skills that are essential for technical students to be active in the global community. The materials will be introduced throughout the units following various situations that the main character, Ken, experiences. Just as English will expand the world for Ken, who lacks confidence in his English ability, so too will English open your future potential.

グローバル化が進む中、異なるバックグラウンドを持つ研究者と英語で協働し研究を進めたり、成果を世界に発信したりする能力は、重要な鍵となります。一方で、理工系を専門とする皆さんの中には、英語に苦手意識を持つ方も少なくないでしょう。

本書は、そんな理工系学生がグローバル社会で活躍するために欠かせない英語力の向上を目的とした学習書です。本書の主人公 Ken の体験を通して、様々な場面に応じて必要な英語を紹介していきます。英語が苦手だった Ken の世界がどんどん広がったように、きっと英語は、皆さんの将来の可能性を大きく広げることでしょう。

Goals of this textbook

✔ Gain the ability to work on collaborative research with people from different backgrounds using English.

✔ Be able to produce academic results in English, such as presentations and research papers.

✔ Develop a positive attitude towards understanding and respecting different cultures.

✔ Become confident in expanding your global network with those in specialized fields, as well as widen your perspective and communication skills.

✔ Overcome your anxiety of English output communication by learning useful expressions and frequently-used vocabulary.

✔ 英語を使い異なるバックグラウンドを持った人々と協働しながら研究を遂行できる。

✔ 英語で研究成果（プレゼンテーションや論文など）をアウトプットできる。

✔ 異文化を理解し、尊重する姿勢を持つことができる。

✔ 専門分野のみならず幅広い視野とコミュニケーション能力で、グローバルに人脈を広げることができる。

✔ 英語でのコミュニケーションに対する苦手意識を克服することができる。

Features of this textbook
✔ Technical Vocabulary required in the fields of engineering and science
✔ Academic Vocabulary frequently used in professional papers and articles
✔ Useful Expressions that are valuable for daily life and beneficial for research and study abroad opportunities

✔ 理工系分野で必要な Technical Vocabulary
✔ 論文等で頻出する Academic Vocabulary
✔ 日常生活や海外留学、研究を進める上で知っておくと便利な Useful Expression

About the listening exercises

 Listen to the audio and answer the questions.
オーディオを聴いて解きましょう。

Story
    Ken begins the textbook with little confidence in his English ability. However, he develops an interest in English and different cultures while supporting John, an international student from Singapore. Ken then gets the opportunity to further interact with people from different backgrounds and broaden his perspective by participating in a short-term study abroad program, as well as attending a workshop, international conference, internship, and more. Over time, he gradually overcomes his English weaknesses and increases his confidence. Let's learn various necessary English words and expressions while experiencing several types of interactions with Ken!

    Ken は、英語が苦手でしたが、シンガポールからの留学生、John のサポート役を担当したことがきっかけで、他国の文化や言語に興味を持ち始めます。その後、海外研修やワークショップ、インターンシップなどへの参加を通して、異なるバックグラウンドを持つ人々と交流し、自分の研究分野に囚われない視野を広げ、少しずつ英語の苦手意識を克服していきます。
    Ken と一緒に様々なコミュニケーション場面を体験しながら、そこで必要な英語を学んでいきましょう！

Main Characters

Ken Nakamura

Ken is a first-year master's student majoring in Management of Technology (MOT) within the Department of Engineering at Osaka Tech University. He's originally from Osaka and is interested in meeting new people and engaging in different projects beyond his research field.

John

John is an international student from Singapore who will be studying abroad at Osaka Tech University for six months. He is also studying Japanese during his free time so that he will have a more fulfilling experience in Japan.

Lin

Lin is a first-year master's student from China who studies Ocean Engineering within the Department of Engineering at Osaka Tech University. She likes to join various projects with people from different backgrounds.

Contents

Introduction i

Goals of this textbook i

Features of this textbook ii

About the listening exercises ii

Story ii

Main Characters iii

Unit *1* Welcoming an International Student 1
Designing and Modeling

INTRODUCTION: LET'S MEET KEN 1

EMAIL EXCHANGE 3

MEETING THE EXCHANGE STUDENT 6

KEN'S RESEARCH 7

DESIGN CONCEPT 10

Unit *2* Welcoming an International Student 2
Static and Dynamic Principles

INTRODUCTION: WORKING IN A LAB 15

SAFETY PROCEDURES IN THE LAB 18

LEARNING ABOUT STATIC PRINCIPLES 22

LEARNING ABOUT DYNAMIC PRINCIPLES 25

A WELCOME DINNER FOR THE NEW LAB MEMBERS 28

Unit *3* Joining a Short-term Study Abroad Program 1
Electricity

INTRODUCTION: APPLYING FOR A STUDY ABROAD PROGRAM 31

ARRIVING AT HIS DESTINATION: TALKING WITH HIS HOST FAMILY 32

ATTENDING A SEMINAR: BASICS OF ELECTRICITY 35

ATTENDING A SEMINAR: THE WORLD-FAMOUS INVENTOR 38

WATCHING THE NEWS ABOUT ELECTRIC CARS 40

Unit *4* Joining a Short-term Study Abroad Program 2
Energy and Temperature

INTRODUCTION: SENDING AN EMAIL TO A PROFESSOR 45

PREPARATION FOR THE LAB VISIT: ENERGY AND TEMPERATURE 48

PREPARATION FOR THE LAB VISIT: KINETIC ENERGY 49

VISITING PROFESSOR BROWN'S LAB: MEETING A STUDENT 53

DISCUSSION: RENEWABLE ENERGY 57

Unit *5* Attending a Workshop
Computing and Future Technology

INTRODUCTION: ATTENDING A WORKSHOP 61

PREPARING FOR THE WORKSHOP 65

DISCUSSION: ARTIFICIAL INTELLIGENCE PREDICTIONS 69

PRESENTATION: ARTIFICIAL INTELLIGENCE PREDICTIONS 71

Unit *6* Student Club Activities
Measurements and Mechanisms

INTRODUCTION: THE BACKGROUND OF A COMPETITION 75

AN ADVERTISEMENT FOR AN ENGINEERING COMPETITION 77

DOING THE MEASUREMENTS I: DRAWING UP THE BLUEPRINTS 81

WORKING TOGETHER TO PLAN THE PROJECT 84

DOING THE MEASUREMENTS II: ACCURACY 86

LEARNING ABOUT MECHANISMS 87

COMPETING IN THE EVENT 89

Unit *7* Touring a Shipyard
Fluid and Air Dynamics

INTRODUCTION: TAKING A CLASS 93

PREPARING FOR THE TOUR: SAFETY TIPS 95

UNDERSTANDING FLUID AND AIR DYNAMICS 96

THE CLASS TOURS A SHIPYARD 101

LEARNING ABOUT CORPORATE SOCIAL RESPONSIBILITY (CSR) 103

FOLLOWING A GOVERNMENT-INITIATED PROJECT: i-Shipping 105

Unit 8 **Visiting Companies**
Manufacturing, Assembly, and Components

INTRODUCTION: PARTICIPATING IN A SPECIAL PROGRAM 109

ATTENDING A LECTURE: BASICS OF MACHINING 111

LEARNING JOINING TECHNIQUES AT A COMPANY 115

UNDERSTANDING THE BACKGROUND: SMART MANUFACTURING 117

VISITING A STEEL COMPANY 121

WORKING ON A PROJECT AT THE COMPANY 123

Unit 9 **Joining an International Conference**
Materials Science

INTRODUCTION: RECEIVING AN EMAIL FROM JOHN 127

BACKGROUND SEARCHING: FINDING A CONFERENCE TO ATTEND 129

SIGNING UP FOR A CONFERENCE 131

PREPARING FOR A POSTER PRESENTATION 136

GIVING A PRESENTATION 140

WATCHING A PLENARY 142

Unit 10 **Applying for an Internship**
Biotechnology and Applied Chemistry

INTRODUCTION: THINKING ABOUT FUTURE CAREERS 145

BACKGROUND SEARCHING: BASICS OF POLYMERS 148

FINDING AN INTERNSHIP TO JOIN 150

PREPARING FOR AN INTERNSHIP 153

JOB INTERVIEW 157

LISTENING SCRIPT 161

ANSWERS 183

KEYWORDS 197

Acknowledgments 205

About the authors 206

Designing and Modeling

INTRODUCTION   LET'S MEET KEN

Hi! I'm Ken!

 Listen to Ken's introduction and circle the correct information.

Ken	Information
1. From	The United States, Japan, Singapore
2. University Major	Aerodynamics, Management, Management of Technology
3. Hobby	Tennis, Soccer, Traveling
4. Plan for next week	Go to Singapore, Meet an exchange student, Travel to Guam

 Listen again to Ken's introduction while reading along and filling in the blanks.

Meet Ken Nakamura. He is from Japan and is a first-year master's student at Osaka Tech University. Ken's major is Management of Technology, or MOT. **1.** _____ _____ _____ this field? It's a fairly new type of study that combines the business features that are useful within a company with technical knowledge. Additionally, Ken is eager to learn about subjects beyond his research focus to broaden his knowledge.

When Ken is not studying, he really enjoys traveling. However, besides going to Guam as a child, he hasn't traveled outside of Japan. He 2.____ ____ someday travel abroad to different countries, and so he's motivated to improve his English skills so that he can communicate with people from different backgrounds.

3.____ ____ ____, an international student from Singapore will be joining Ken's lab next week. He'll be studying in Japan for six months as part of an exchange program. Ken is 4.____ ____ ____ meeting him and has already volunteered to 5.____ ____ ____ the campus and help him get accustomed to life in Japan.

In this first unit, we'll learn about designing and modeling, which are fundamental steps in creating any new products. Given Ken's major and future interests, he will need to learn them as part of his curriculum.

Let's learn about designing and modeling for a class that Ken is taking.

C Read the passage and write the appropriate words. Some words need to be changed to match the sentences. Not all words are used.

sketch	modification	rough draft	incorporate
	prototype	distribute	

The process of designing and modeling involves a sophisticated approach with multiple steps along the way. It's more than simply copying other designs and making something better through slight 1.____. It's a fundamental, start-to-finish operation that begins with addressing a question. For example: 'How can we 2.____ our customers' needs by making a more fuel-efficient engine?'. Then we define the current and potential problems that may arise, such as 'why haven't others found an answer to this question yet?' and 'what potential issues may we experience that will stop us from creating this product?'. This step can involve several departments of a company coming up with an answer. Instead of focusing on one team's ideas, it is important to collaborate with other experts to gain the input of a variety of employees, such as those with technical competencies like engineers, as well as people in the business and administrative sides. This collaboration is important for developing a **3.**_____, which is a first, imperfect version of a product that includes simple drawings, or **4.**_____. These can be done by hand or even with 3D software known as Computer-Aided Design (CAD). Eventually, a **5.**_____ is developed, which is a functional but unfinished model of a product. Products often undergo modifications over and over again in order to avoid being recalled in the future. In fact, even after they have been finished and released for sale, it is still important to make updated versions in the future.

D Refer to *C* and circle all of the parts in the box that are related to designing and modeling.

The steps in designing and modeling include:

Ex.) (Addressing a question)	1. Copying a previous design	2. Defining the problems
3. Focusing on one team's ideas	4. Collaborating with technical and business people	5. Creating an advertisement
6. Developing a prototype	7. Recalling the finished product	8. Undergoing modifications

| EMAIL EXCHANGE

Ken received an email from John, the international exchange student from Singapore.

Read the email and change the order of the expressions.

To: Ken Nakamura

From: John

Dear Ken,

It's nice to meet you. My name is John, and I am an exchange student from Singapore.

I am writing this email to you today because I will be studying at your lab next month. I was given your email address and was told that you volunteered to give me some assistance, so I hope it is OK to contact you directly. I really appreciate your help, by the way.

1. (to / give / me / allow / some) background information about myself. I am a first-year master's student, and I'm majoring in physics. I've never traveled outside my country before and am both very excited and nervous to come to Japan. I hope to have a great experience!

2. (I / if / we / was / wondering) could meet sometime when you are free. I can't speak Japanese, so I hope it's OK if we communicate in English. After arriving, I will need to check into my dorm and get situated. Therefore, I can't meet you in person on that day. But **3.** (meet you / I'd / to / be happy) any day after that. Just let me know when and where you'd like to meet. I'm fine with whatever works for you.

4. (seeing you / I / look / forward to) soon.

Regards,
John

---

1. to / give / me / allow / some

2. I / if / we / was / wondering

3. meet you / I'd / to / be happy

4. seeing you / I / look / forward to

B Write a response to John's email below. Hint: Try using the useful expressions (1-4) in **A** .

To: John

From: Ken Nakamura

Dear John,

1. [greeting and introduction] _____

_____

_____

2. [background information about Ken] _____

_____

_____

3. [answer to John's request] _____

_____

4. [closing comment] _____

_____

Regards,
Ken

C Listen to some things that an exchange student might ask or say to you. Choose the most appropriate response.

1. (a) (b) (c)   2. (a) (b) (c)

3. (a) (b) (c)   4. (a) (b) (c)

MEETING THE EXCHANGE STUDENT

Ken and John are meeting each other for the first time.

  Listen to the conversation and number the pictures in order.

1ˢᵗ _____ ⟹ 2ⁿᵈ _____ ⟹ 3ʳᵈ _____ ⟹ 4ᵗʰ _____ ⟹ 5ᵗʰ _____

B Listen to the audio and write what you hear. Then compare your sentences with a partner. Finally, check your answers.

1. _____
   _____

2. _____
   _____

3. _____
   _____

4. _____
   _____

KEN'S RESEARCH

Let's learn more about Ken's major and research.

  Read the passage about Management of Technology and choose the appropriate words.

There has traditionally been a divide between people with **1.** (technical / ethnical / ethical) expertise and those with business skills. Previously, people were **2.** (forgotten / considered / gone) to be either in technical or non-technical positions. Some people were strictly businessmen who managed employees or sold products to customers, while others were engineers or scientists who focused on more specific things such as working out the proportions of a skyscraper building or discovering new vaccines. However, there are **3.** (opportunities / constraints / connections) when focusing on only technical or practical skills. In other words, this type of thinking creates limitations for learning a broad range of important competencies. We are now starting to understand the importance of being able to understand both sides. For example, a business person can benefit from understanding the technical needs of his/her engineering department. Likewise, an engineer should have the ability to visualize what customers actually want in order to create the best product. Therefore, the **4.** (incorporation / affection / fiction) of several competencies into one major is a trend that many universities are following in today's world.

  Listen to more information about Management of Technology and answer the questions.

1. What does **'complements'** mean in the following sentence?: *"Management of Technology complements technical knowledge with business features."*
    (a) People who study MOT will receive lots of praise.
    (b) MOT offers more than technical knowledge; it also includes business knowledge.
    (c) MOT became more important than business knowledge.

2. What is the benefit of choosing a master's degree in Management of Technology?
    (a) Students can focus solely on business after completing their undergraduate degree.
    (b) Students can focus exclusively on engineering after they have completed their business degree.
    (c) Students can learn both engineering and business competencies.

Ken's research focus is on designing robots for fulfillment centers to help with tasks that humans must currently do. Let's learn some background information on fulfillment centers to understand his research better.

 Listen to the process of a fulfillment center and put the pictures in order from the first step to the last.

(a) place an order

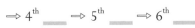

1st (a) ⇒ 2nd _____ ⇒ 3rd _____

⇒ 4th _____ ⇒ 5th _____ ⇒ 6th _____

(b) send boxes down

(c) receive an instruction

(d) gather/pack

(e) distribute to customers

(f) load onto trucks

Listen again to the audio from $\boxed{C}$ **and discuss the following with a partner.**

1. Which steps in the fulfillment center process are done by using robots? Which steps need humans to complete?
2. Choose a step that you think can be achieved by robots. Explain how robots can accomplish this task.
3. Do you think robots will someday replace human workers completely? Explain.

DESIGN CONCEPT

 Match the English vocabulary with the correct definition.

Ex.) analyze   (a) the importance of something

1. distribute   (b) a series of steps taken to achieve a goal or purpose

2. formula   (c) a math rule shown in symbols, or a system for doing something

3. process   (d) to give something to others or to spread something around

4. significance   (e) to study something in detail

5. proposal   (f) something that offers a new idea

Ken and John are now looking at the flyer for the design concept competition.

B Read the event information and answer the questions.

Design Concept Competition

Are you interested in creating a new design concept? Would you like to compete for a grand prize? If so, join our competition on July 31st for a chance to win! Contestants can choose to submit all types of concepts using any design process of their choice (computer-generated models, written blueprints, etc.). You can either choose to make improvements to an existing product or even create something entirely new. Best of all, the theme can be anything you want, so feel free to get creative!

A panel of volunteer judges will grade designs based on a number of factors, including creativity and the incorporation of new approaches and ways of thinking.

1st place: a travel package to a domestic spa resort, including food and lodging
2nd place: an MP3 player
3rd place: a gift card to your favorite store

Please note:
- In-person registration is not allowed, and only proposals submitted in advance will be accepted into the competition. To register, visit our website, select 'participate' and fill out and submit the registration form for pre-approval. Once you receive a confirmation email, submit your proposal via email to: prototypesub@univ.mail.co.jp. Be sure to include your name, confirmation number, and student ID.
- While we are sure that many people would like to take part in this event, participation is limited to current students of Osaka Tech University. Therefore, only the prototypes created by university-affiliated students will be permitted.

---

1. What are the most important factors for designs to be graded highly?
   (a) using creativity to create a durable and high-performing product
   (b) being creative and including new approaches and ways of thinking
   (c) making improvements to an existing model and being creative

2. What is the process for registering and submitting?
   (a) First, submit a proposal. Then go to the organization's website and register.
   (b) First, submit the registration form for pre-approval via the organization's website. Then submit a proposal after receiving a confirmation email.
   (c) First, register in person and pay the fee. Then wait for approval.

3. Who can participate in the competition?
    (a) only current students of Ken's university
    (b) anyone that registers and pays the fee
    (c) students of local universities

4. What information does the flyer NOT include?
    (a) participation eligibility
    (b) the website's address
    (c) information on how to register

Ken and John are planning on submitting a proposal for the design concept competition!

 C Read part of Ken and John's proposal and answer the questions.

Proposal Concept: A new revolutionary bicycle

Bicycles are useful in our daily lives for both convenience and recreational activities. They come in many different sizes and usually include a frame, two wheels, a seat, pedals, and handlebars. While the design of bicycles has changed dramatically since their invention, they continue to have the same constraints. That is, they are usually large and heavy, and they require a place to park when not being used. Because of this, bicycles are not a feasible transportation solution for many people. A large focus of bike development has centered on the design considerations of speed and weight, given the large market for competitive racing. While having a lightweight and fast bike can benefit commuters, it still does not alleviate the original drawbacks.

Therefore, our proposal is a new type of bicycle that will resolve the abovementioned constraints. This bicycle will mostly cater to active people who need fast and convenient transportation, but do not have access to bicycle parking lots or do not want to carry a heavy bike. To accomplish this, our design focuses on the bicycle being both lightweight and portable. By incorporating new state-of-the-art lightweight and durable metals, and by redesigning various parts, we can lower the overall weight and size. Also when the bike needs to be carried, its frame and small wheels fold into a compact circle. The bike can then fit into a special backpack and be carried for easy transportation. Best of all, the backpack also doubles as a front cargo basket to carry items when riding the bike.

For additional information, please see the attached design concept blueprints.

1. What are the main constraints of traditional bicycles? _____

_____

2. What type of bicycle do they propose to create? _____

_____

3. What design considerations did they think about?
    (a) budget   (b) style and appeal   (c) weight and portability

4. Which bicycle are they describing?

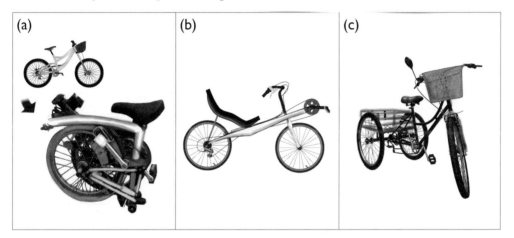

 Work with a partner and discuss the remaining two prototype pictures from *C*. Answer the questions.

1. What do you think is the purpose of each bike?
2. What design considerations were considered for each one? Example: speed, price, style, etc.
3. What new bike concept would you like to create? What purpose would it have?

While Ken and John's design concept was an interesting idea, their proposal did not place in the top three, so they did not receive a prize. At least they had fun working on it together.

Static and Dynamic Principles

| INTRODUCTION WORKING IN A LAB

Let's learn about static and dynamic principles while helping John in the lab!

  Listen to Ken's update while reading. Circle the words you hear.

In this unit, Ken will help John get accustomed to his new lab. Alongside this, Ken will also learn about static and dynamic principles, which are related to John's physics major. Specifically, he'll learn about different types of forces that push against immobile objects like bridges as they try to bear **1.** (roads / loads / codes). He'll also learn about the forces that push against moving objects like rockets, drones, and planes. It sounds like a lot of fun! **2.** (Whether it is addressed / Whenever I guess / Nevertheless), in order to **3.** (pure / ensure / cure) that John can **4.** (conduct / deduct / product) experiments in the lab, Ken must first help him gain **5.** (sufficient / efficient / ancient) knowledge about the rules, regulations, and safety procedures. Of course, Ken is looking forward to helping John out in this regard.

B Listen to the audio. Circle the correct type of body for each picture.

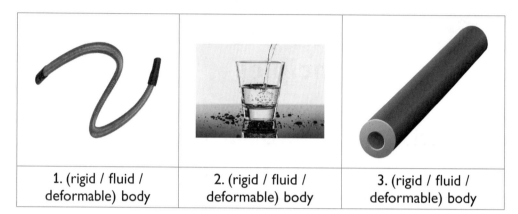

| 1. (rigid / fluid / deformable) body | 2. (rigid / fluid / deformable) body | 3. (rigid / fluid / deformable) body |

 C Now read the explanation and write rigid, deformable, or fluid.

1. This object cannot move or bend and instead stays solid. If you apply too much force, it will just break and cannot return to its original structure.
This is a _____ body.

2. This object is not a solid body. It's a liquid that moves like water in a melted state.
This is a _____ body.

3. This object has the ability to bend without breaking. If you stop putting force on it, it should return to its original structure.
This is a _____ body.

Ken is now learning about static and dynamic force. Let's learn what the differences are!

Listen and read while filling in the blanks with the words you hear from the box.

dynamic	velocity	static	bear a load
	acceleration	rigid	friction

Imagine a support beam for a house like the picture on the left. The purpose of the beam is to hold the house up and support the weight of the walls and roof; it must **1.**_____.

To *bear something* means to hold its weight. And a *load* is just an object that is being carried. But the building is very heavy, and it puts substantial weight onto the support beam. If there is too much weight, the support beam will bend or even break. The force that pushes on an object that is not in motion is called **2.**_____ force. The support beam must balance this force while remaining still.

Now imagine a rocket flying in the air like the picture on the left. Unlike the house support beam, this rocket is moving fast. While it's in motion, there is a force pushing against it. The force that pushes against a moving object is called **3.**_____ force. As you can imagine, more parameters are needed to calculate where the rocket will travel. Such parameters include **4.**_____, which measures how fast something is moving in a certain direction. There's also **5.**_____, the increase in speed within a certain amount of time. We also need to measure the resistance that an object has when rubbing against another object, which is known as **6.**_____.

Now, while the support beam and rocket have different forces acting on them, they are both considered **7.**_____ bodies. This means that they are not supposed to bend, break, or melt when forces push against them.

E Look at the information again in **D** and circle the correct words in the chart below.

1. **Static force** = (rocket / support beam) 2. The object (is / isn't) a rigid body. 3. The object (is / isn't) moving. 4. We (do / don't) need to calculate parameters for movement.	5. **Dynamic force** = (rocket / support beam) 6. The object (is / isn't) a rigid body. 7. The object (is / isn't) moving. 8. We (do / don't) need to calculate parameters for movement.

SAFETY PROCEDURES IN THE LAB

John must learn about the lab safety procedures before he can conduct any experiments.

 A Choose the letter for the appropriate word with the same meaning of the boldfaced words.

> (a) not allowed   (b) therefore   (c) rough
> (d) however   (e) discuss

1. There are a few things that I have to **go over** first before we proceed. _____
2. Working in a lab can have certain risks. **Nevertheless**, hazards can be avoided. _____
3. Safety procedures are important; **hence**, we must understand them. _____
4. The results came from an **approximate** measurement, meaning it was not exact.

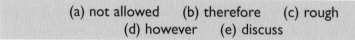

5. The use of cellphones is **prohibited** while in the lab. Please refrain from doing so.

(f) you need to	(g) situation	(h) ends
(i) as a general rule	(j) be aware	

6. Depending on the **circumstances**, you may be asked to stay late while conducting your experiment. _____

7. This **concludes** the lecture. Are there any questions? _____

8. **Keep in mind** that our supply is limited. _____

9. **Make sure to** read this before the class. _____

10. **In principle**, materials will be available for free. _____

 Listen to the professor's lecture. Write a checkmark (√) for the items that John must bring next week and cross out (✗) the things he doesn't need to bring.

THINGS TO BRING NEXT WEEK	√ / ✗
1. shoes with closed toes	
2. steel-toed boots	
3. lab coat	
4. safety goggles	
5. respirator mask	
6. vinyl gloves	

C Here is a section of the lab rules. Read it and complete the sentences by choosing the most appropriate answer.

Lab Rules

Dear students,

Please read the lab rules carefully and make sure that you understand them. If you have any questions or concerns regarding the following, please see me during office hours.

To ensure your safety and the safety of your classmates, I have established a list of lab rules that everyone must abide by. While working in a lab is considered relatively safe, it is important that you understand that there are potential risks involved. For us to minimize these risks, each student will be required to read the following rules and show sufficient understanding before any experiments can be conducted. Failure to adhere to any of these safety procedures will be considered as a violation of the lab rules, resulting in the student not being permitted to participate in lab activities.

[...]

According to the above lab rules:

Ex.) If you have any questions, … ———	a. see the professor during office hours.
	b. send the professor an email.

1. Rules have been created …	a. to guarantee students' safety.
	b. to address frequent questions.

2. Working in a lab is safe, but …	a. a professor still needs to be present.
	b. we should be aware of possible risks.

3. Students must first review and show …	a. that they understand the rules.
	b. that they have signed the lab rules.

4. Students who do not follow the rules …	a. will receive a warning.
	b. will not be able to participate.

John is asking Ken some questions regarding the lab rules.

 Listen to the conversation and circle the permissible things. Write an X for things that are not allowed and leave unmentioned items blank.

Lab Rules

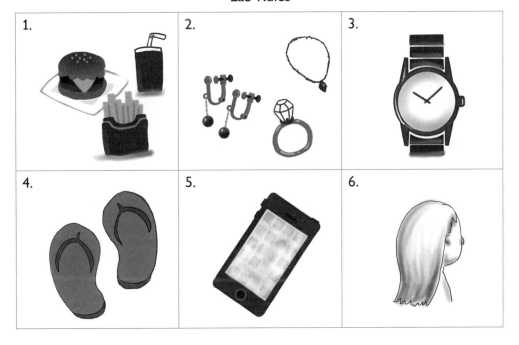

LEARNING ABOUT STATIC PRINCIPLES

The class is learning about structural failure.

 Read the description of failure and answer the questions.

Professor:

Let's talk about failure. Failure is when something that is bearing a load, or holding the weight of an object, fails to maintain that weight and deforms or breaks. Think of a rigid body like a building's pillar. You don't want the pillar to move, right? But there can be a lot of heavy static forces pressing on it from different directions. If all forces pushing against the pillar are countered and equalized, meaning the pillar balances the pressure against it perfectly, we call it equilibrium. But if the pillar can't balance the enormous forces and ends up breaking, we call this failure.

Now, we learned about static force and dynamic force, but what is 'force'? And what is the difference between stress and force? They sound similar, right? Well, stress is an object's own ability to resist change. Therefore, we are focusing on the object that is receiving the pressure. Force is the opposite. It is the pressure that is pushing or pulling on objects. So, an object receives stress from an outside force.

1. How does failure occur?
   (a) when all forces are balanced and equilibrium is achieved
   (b) when a measurement is not calculated correctly and must be fixed
   (c) when something has too much stress and loses its ability to bear the forces pushing against it

2. What is equilibrium?
   (a) Equilibrium is the situation where an object fails to bear a load and breaks.
   (b) Equilibrium is the state where the forces pushing against an object are countered and equalized.
   (c) Equilibrium is when an object deforms due to an equalized force.

3. What is the difference between stress and force?

   (a) Stress and force both receive pressure, but force is stronger.

   (b) Force is the pressure that an object receives. Stress is the pressure pushing on an object.

   (c) Stress is the pressure that an object receives. Force is the pressure pushing on an object.

 B **Complete the sentences by drawing a line to the appropriate definitions.**

Ex.) 'Bearing' something means … ——— (a) to carry its weight.

1. A load is …

2. Stress is …

3. Force is …

4. A dynamic object is …

5. A static object is …

6. Failure occurs when …

7. Equilibrium occurs when …

(b) an object that doesn't move.

(c) an object undergoes stress and deforms or breaks.

(d) the forces pushing against an object are balanced.

(e) the object being carried.

(f) an object that moves.

(g) the internal resistance of a body that's receiving pressure.

(h) something pushing or pulling on an object.

There are several different ways that forces can cause failure. Let's learn about them.

C Match the definitions of different forces with the pictures.

1. **Tension**: the force that pulls on an object, trying to stretch and make it longer ___

2. **Torque**: the force that twists an object in a circular motion ___

3. **Shearing**: the force that puts pressure in two opposite directions, making the object cut into two pieces ___

4. **Bending**: the force that flexes and bends an object, morphing it into a curve or angled shape ___

5. **Compression**: the force that pushes an object inward, flattening it ___

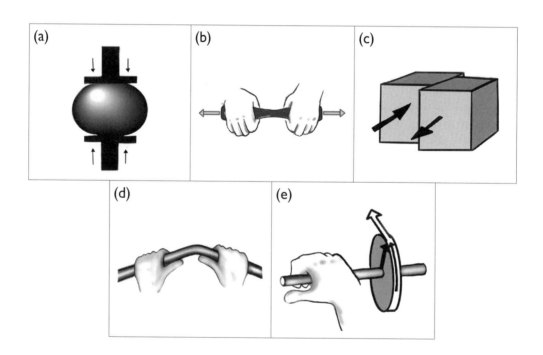

(a) (b) (c) (d) (e)

LEARNING ABOUT DYNAMIC PRINCIPLES

After the lecture, Ken became curious about dynamic principles and looked up some information about drones.

 Here is part of an article that Ken found about drones. Read it and select the appropriate words from the box below.

> decelerate   pivot   accelerate   velocity

Have you ever had the chance to fly a drone before? Or maybe you have seen them buzzing around your local park. Drones have become increasingly popular over the last ten years. But what do you think is the appeal? Well, one of the advantages of drones is their low weight and small size. Because of this, they can **1.**_____ very fast. This means that they can go from zero, or not moving, to top speed very quickly. Drones' top **2.**_____ is also pretty high considering how inexpensive they are. Now, how fast can a drone fly? Well, that depends on a number of factors such as the power of its engine and how much it weighs. An inexpensive drone may be only able to fly at 30KPH, while some of the fastest types can fly at over 300KPH.

Drones can also quickly **3.**_____, meaning they can slow down. Best of all, they have the ability to swiftly **4.**_____, or make sharp and sudden turns. Compared to a conventional aircraft or helicopter, a drone's ability to turn sharply is astounding.

$\mathcal{B}$ Match the appropriate words with the pictures.

decelerate   pivot   accelerate   top velocity

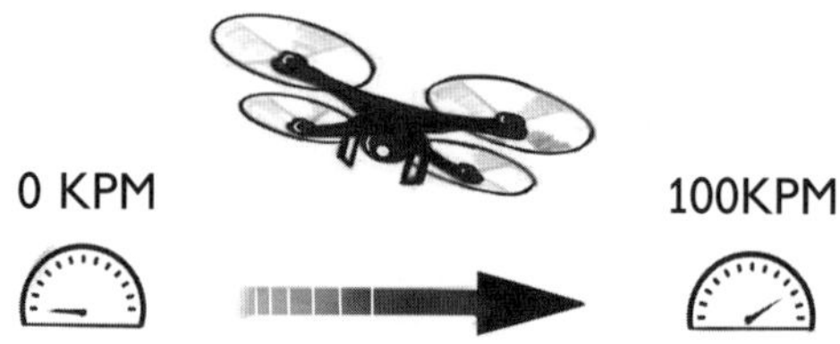

0 KPM   100KPM

1. _____

100KPH   20KPH

2. _____

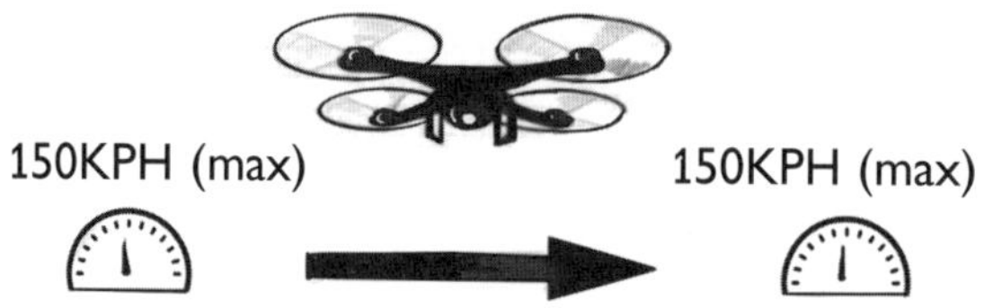

150KPH (max)   150KPH (max)

3. _____

4. _____

C Look at the comparison chart between the drone and helicopter and answer the questions.

Model: T200 RC Drone	Model: Rescue Copter 1

Description: unmanned RC drone

Avg. revolutions per minute (RPM): ~20,000

Acceleration: high

Deceleration: very high

Pivoting: high

Maximum carrying capacity: very low

Top velocity: medium

Average cost: very inexpensive
¥¥

Description: manned helicopter, 5 passengers

Avg. revolutions per minute (RPM): ~440

Acceleration: medium

Deceleration: medium

Pivoting: medium

Maximum carrying capacity: high

Top velocity: high

Average cost: very expensive
¥¥¥¥¥¥

Ex.)　Which can maneuver quicker? Why?　<u>The drone can maneuver quicker than the</u> <u>helicopter because its pivoting ability is higher.</u>

1.　Which can bear a higher load? _____

2.　Which can start and stop moving faster? Why? _____

_____

3.　In what situation would you use a drone? Why? _____

_____

4.　In what situation would you use a manned helicopter? Why? _____

_____

A WELCOME DINNER FOR THE NEW LAB MEMBERS

Ken and his lab mates are planning a welcome dinner for John and other exchange students.

Read Ken's invitation letter and choose the answer with a similar meaning to the boldfaced words.

Invitation Letter

Dear all,

    We are planning on hosting a dinner next Friday for all of the incoming students. Hopefully, you will be able to **1. stop by** and enjoy some good food and conversation with your new classmates. The location will be at the campus restaurant. The doors will open at 18:00, but **2. feel free** to arrive any time after.

    For those of you who have volunteered to help host the event, we'll be having a meeting this Wednesday to **3. go over** the plans. Please join if you have time.

    Well, **4. that's about it**. If you have any questions, **5. you can reach me** at (080) XXX-XXXX.

See you there!

Ken

1. **stop by** and enjoy some good food
   (a) leave   (b) arrive on time   (c) come

2. **feel free** to arrive any time
   (a) there's no fee   (b) there's no pressure   (c) it would be good

3. **go over** the plans
   (a) discuss   (b) submit   (c) discontinue

4. **that's about it**
   (a) it's correct   (b) there's nothing more to say   (c) let's talk about it

5. you can **reach me**
   (a) contact me   (b) see me   (c) leave me

B Read some sentences that were said before and during the dinner and unscramble the words.

1. "There will be many people attending, so there may not be any food left if we arrive too late."
   "Well, let's arrive much earlier ____ ____ ____ ____ gets crowded."

   (a) in   (b) it   (c) case   (d) just

2. "Hi, I'm here for the lab dinner."
   "OK, great. ____ ____ ____ ____ show you to your table."

   (a) be   (b) to   (c) happy   (d) I'll

3. "I look forward to working with you on the project later this week. We should talk soon."
   "____ ____ ____ ____ my contact information. Please call me sometime."

   (a) me   (b) let   (c) give   (d) you

4. I understand that you are new in the lab and don't know some things. Don't worry. I can assist you at any time. If you need anything, ____ ____ ____ ____ me for help.

   (a) ask   (b) feel   (c) to   (d) free

C Listen to the speaker and choose the best response.

1. (a) (b) (c)   2. (a) (b) (c)   3. (a) (b) (c)

4. (a) (b) (c)   5. (a) (b) (c)

> The dinner went well and everyone had a great time getting to know each other.

unit 3

Electricity

> After having a good time with John, Ken is now taking a big step!

INTRODUCTION
APPLYING FOR A STUDY ABROAD PROGRAM

 A Listen to Ken's study abroad plan and answer the questions.

1. Where will Ken go to study abroad?
   (a) South America
   (b) The United States
   (c) Guam

2. When will Ken study abroad?
   (a) From August 1st to August 30th
   (b) From August 1st to August 13th
   (c) From August 1st to August 21st

3. What is Ken's main purpose for studying abroad?
   (a) To conduct his research
   (b) To broaden his perspective
   (c) To improve his English

4. What is Ken's concern regarding studying abroad?

    (a) He thinks his English is not good enough to communicate with the local people.

    (b) He thinks he will miss his family.

    (c) He thinks he might get lost in a foreign country.

 Answer the questions and then discuss them with a partner.

1. Which country would you like to study abroad at? Why?

_____

2. What activities would you like to do if you study abroad?

_____

3. What concerns do you have about studying abroad?

_____

ARRIVING AT HIS DESTINATION
TALKING WITH HIS HOST FAMILY

After arriving in the U.S., Ken is having his first breakfast with his host family.

Read the conversation with a partner. Then choose the closest meanings to the boldfaced words.

Host Father : **1. Make yourself at home.**

Ken   : Thank you. I appreciate you letting me stay with you.

Host Father : **2. Don't mention it.** Have you overcome your jetlag yet?

Ken   : Not yet. I couldn't sleep until late last night.

Host Father : That's too bad. I hope you won't be too sleepy. So, what's your plan for today?

Ken   : Well, I'm thinking about attending a seminar on business and innovations at the university. They'll introduce the history of Thomas Edison. I'm curious about how he could be such a great inventor and businessman at the same time. But I'm not sure if I am confident enough with my English to attend it.

Host Father : Oh, don't worry about it! **3. Why don't you just go ahead and try?**

Ken   : Yeah, you're right. I probably should. Well, **4. wish me luck!**

Host Father : Of course! Alright, breakfast is ready. **5. Help yourself!**

---

1. Make yourself at home.
   (a) Please be responsible.
   (b) Please help us.
   (c) Please be relaxed.

2. Don't mention it.
   (a) You're welcome.
   (b) I don't like it.
   (c) It's all yours.

3. Why don't you just go ahead and try?
   (a) You should do it.
   (b) Please start eating.
   (c) Why are you going?

4. Wish me luck!
   (a) I feel lucky today.
   (b) Please wish me success.
   (c) I am usually lucky.

5. Help yourself.
   (a) Please help me.
   (b) Please feel free to eat.
   (c) Please take care of yourself.

B Here are some questions you may be asked if you go on a homestay. Practice asking and answering them with a partner.

1. What do you like to do in your spare time?
2. What is college life like in Japan?
3. What are your plans for the future?
4. What kind of research do you do?
5. Why did you choose your research topic?

C If you were staying at Ken's host family's house, what questions would you ask the family? Write three questions and compare them with a partner.

Ex.) What do you know about Japan?

1.

2.

3.

ATTENDING A SEMINAR   BASICS OF ELECTRICITY

Ken will attend a seminar on business and innovations and learn about the history of Thomas Edison, the world-famous inventor and successful businessman. Before the seminar, he'll review some vocabulary related to electricity.

 Here is the International System of Units for electricity. Choose the correct words from the box and fill in the blanks.

| magnetic flux | siemens | electromotive force | farad |
| electrical charge | electrical resistance | magnetic flux density | henry |

Type of electricity		Name	Symbol
1. _____		volt	V
2. _____		ohm	Ω
3. _____		coulomb	C
electrical conductance	4. _____		S
capacitance	5. _____		F
inductance	6. _____		H
7. _____		weber	Wb
8. _____		tesla	T

B Read the explanation about AC versus DC power and choose the right vocabulary from the box to fill in the blanks.

alternating	transmit	direct	circuits
voltage	utilized	transformer	

There are two types of currents used in most electronic **1.**＿＿＿＿＿＿＿ across the world; they are called alternating current (AC) and direct current (DC).

2.＿＿＿＿＿＿＿ current has a constant flow of electric charge moving in one direction and is typically low **3.**＿＿＿＿＿＿＿ electricity. Batteries generate this type of electricity to power things like handheld electronic devices. Also, most electronics use this type of current for their power by changing AC to DC using a **4.**＿＿＿＿＿＿＿.

5.＿＿＿＿＿＿＿ current has a flow of electric charge that is constantly changing directions depending on its frequency, which is typically at 50 or 60 Hertz and is high voltage. This current is mostly **6.**＿＿＿＿＿＿＿ nowadays to **7.**＿＿＿＿＿＿＿ power through power lines. In West Japan, the standard frequency that the current alternates at is 50 Hertz. In East Japan, it is 60 Hertz.

C Use the information in **B** to guess which illustration is alternating current and direct current. Write them in the blanks below.

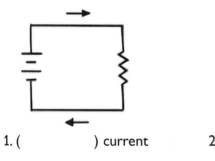

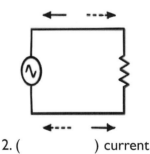

1. (＿＿＿＿＿) current   2. (＿＿＿＿＿) current

D Read about semiconductors and answer the questions.

(a)	Semiconductors have impacted our lives in many ways and are considered the most important parts for all microprocessor chips and transistors in the world. If something is computerized or emits radio waves, then it surely requires semiconductors. They are used for manufacturing many kinds of electronic devices, including transistors, diodes, and computer circuits.
(b)	Semiconductors have a conductivity between things that conduct electricity, such as metals, and nonconductors or insulators, such as ceramics. They can be pure elements such as silicon or germanium, or compounds such as cadmium selenide or gallium arsenide. Through a process called doping, small amounts of impurities are added to pure semiconductors. This causes large changes in the conductivity of the material.
(c)	There are many benefits of using semiconductors. They are compact, power-efficient, low cost, and reliable. They can also handle currents and voltages well. Overall, semiconductors can be used in complex applications while still remaining a feasible option for everyday household electronics.
(d)	Most semiconductor chips and transistors are made with silicon. I'm sure you've heard the name Silicon Valley, the area south of San Francisco in Northern California, USA, that is considered as the global center for technological innovation. Silicon Valley got its name because silicon is the main ingredient in all electronic devices, and the region first became famous due to having a large amount of silicon chip manufacturers.

1. Which paragraph talks about the world-famous region?   (a) (b) (c) (d)

2. Which paragraph talks about how semiconductors function?   (a) (b) (c) (d)

3. Which paragraph talks about the advantages of semiconductors?

    (a) (b) (c) (d)

4. Which paragraph talks about the importance of semiconductors?

    (a) (b) (c) (d)

ATTENDING A SEMINAR
THE WORLD-FAMOUS INVENTOR

> Ken learned about the story of Thomas Edison at the seminar.

 Draw a line to match the vocabulary with the correct definition.

1. inventor
2. acquire

3. patent
4. driving force
5. innovation
6. manufacturer

(a) the creation of something new and revolutionary
(b) a form of intellectual property that gives the owner certain rights
(c) a person or company that creates goods to sell
(d) a person who creates new things
(e) something that pushes progress forward
(f) to obtain something

 Read the story of Thomas Edison and answer True or False.

Thomas Edison was an American inventor and one of America's leading businessmen. He was born in Milan, Ohio, on February 11th, 1847, and died in New Jersey on October 18th, 1931, at the age of 84. In his lifetime, Edison personally and jointly acquired a record number of 1,093 patents, 389 of which were for electric lights and power, 195 for the phonograph, 150 for the telegraph, 141 for storage batteries, and 34 for the telephone. Additionally, he created the world's first industrial research laboratory. Edison was the driving force behind such innovations as the phonograph, the first commercially viable incandescent light bulb, and one of the earliest motion picture cameras. Surprisingly, Edison received minimal formal education and dropped out of school when he was only 12 and started working on the railroad. Nevertheless, he had a talent for creating new inventions and was a successful manufacturer and businessman with a fantastic ability to market his inventions. By the time Edison was in his 30's, his accomplishments had led him to become one of the most famous men in the world.

1. Edison became an inventor after graduating from college. [True / False]
2. Edison had 1,093 personal patents over his lifetime. [True / False]
3. Edison became famous after the 1930s. [True / False]
4. Edison was not just a great inventor but was also a successful businessman.
[True / False]

 C **Discuss the following questions with your partner.**

1. What kind of problems would we have in our daily lives without electricity?
2. What do you think will be the next greatest electrical invention? Why?
3. What do you think is the most environmentally-friendly way to generate electricity?

Ken also learned that Edison left behind many quotes. He received some inspiration by learning some of them!

 14

D Listen to the quotes and write what you hear. Then compare your answers with the script.

1. _____

2. _____

3. _____

4. _____

E Discuss what the quotes in **D** mean with a partner. Then choose your favorite and explain to your partner why it is your favorite.

Ex.)

"I like No. 1 because…"

"I chose No. 2 since…"

"I agree with the quote from No. 3 because…"

WATCHING THE NEWS ABOUT ELECTRIC CARS

Ken watched the nightly news about electric cars with his host father.

Listen to the news report while reading. Choose the word with a similar meaning.

Reporter:

Good evening. In today's business news, **Ex.) automobile** company Roger stated that they are **1. allocating** an **2. estimated** $400 million towards **3. pursuing** their goal of creating efficient electric vehicles within three years. An electric vehicle, or EV, is an automobile that uses an electric motor as its **4. primary** source of propulsion. The electrical energy for these motors is stored in rechargeable batteries. One of the primary benefits of an EV is the lack of CO_2 emissions. To **5. investigate** further, we collected data on various countries' supply and demand for electric cars. [...]

Ex.) automobile	(a) car	(b) phone	(c) computer
1. allocating	(a) involving	(b) merging	(c) distributing
2. estimated	(a) approximated	(b) exact	(c) unknown
3. pursuing	(a) following	(b) purchasing	(c) avoiding
4. primary	(a) brilliant	(b) sophisticated	(c) main
5. investigate	(a) eliminate	(b) overlook	(c) look into

 The news showed the popularity of electric cars amongst different countries. Look at the graphs and answer the questions.

*Figure: 👤 : 10% of the population   👤 : 5% of the population

Demand for plug-in electric vehicles

1. Which of the following statements is most likely to be true regarding the graph above?

   (a) The graph depicts Japan, Italy, and Korea as having similar popularity regarding electric vehicles.

   (b) The graph depicts Korea and China as being the two most popular electric car countries in Asia.

   (c) The graph depicts Germany as the third most popular country.

   (d) The graph depicts Norway as leading the world in electric vehicle demand, while Spain is shown as having the least demand.

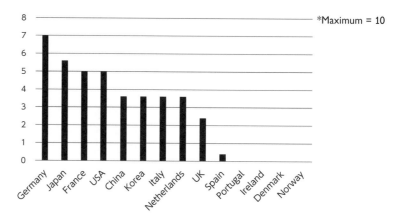

Supply of plug-in electric vehicles

2. Which of the following statements is most likely to be true regarding the graph above?

   (a) Germany is leading in the global supply of plug-in electric vehicles, with Denmark, Portugal, Ireland, and Norway at the bottom.

   (b) Korea's supply of electric cars is less than the UK's supply.

   (c) The supply of electric cars by the Netherlands is less than one-third of Germany's supply.

   (d) Spain has the least supply among European countries.

Afterward, Ken and his host father discussed the topic of electric cars.

Listen to the conversation and fill in the blanks with the words you hear.

Host Father :	Would you like to buy an electric car in the near future?
Ken :	Hmm... **1.**____ ____ ____ the price. In my opinion, they are still too expensive despite their efficiency.
Host Father :	I know what you mean. Oh, **2.**____ ____ the price of electric cars, I read a news article online that was mentioning how the batteries for electric cars will be getting much cheaper in the near future.
Ken :	That would be great.
Host Father :	Right now, you can see electric cars **3.**____ ____ ____. But I believe we'll soon see them everywhere.
Ken :	I would be happy if that happened since electric cars are relatively environmentally friendly.
Host Father :	I agree with you. But I'm sure there are both **4.**____ ____ ____ of driving electric vehicles, don't you think?
Ken :	Well, the downside is that with the technology right now, the distance you can drive on a single charge is somewhat limited.
Host Father :	Yeah, that's definitely a factor to consider. And what about the benefits?
Ken :	**5.**____ ____... From what I know, it will always be cheaper overall, right?
Host Father :	I doubt it. But it really depends on how many miles you put on the car and how long you keep it. If you don't drive much and end up selling the car in a couple of years, then a gas-powered car might be cheaper in the end.
Ken :	That's true.

D Practice useful expressions for stating your opinion. Listen again to certain sentences from **C** and shadow what you hear.

1. In my opinion, they are still too expensive.
2. I believe we'll soon see them everywhere.
3. I agree with you. But I'm sure there are both pros and cons, don't you think?
4. Yeah, that's definitely a factor to consider.
5. From what I know, it will always be cheaper overall, right?
6. I doubt it.

E Discuss the pros and cons of electric cars with your partner. Make a list below.

Pros	Cons
	Ex.) The distance that you can drive on a single charge is limited.

Ken's adventure in America is so far so good!

unit 4

Energy and Temperature

To enhance his study abroad experience, Ken decided to visit a famous laboratory at Rocklin University during his stay in the U.S.!

INTRODUCTION
SENDING AN EMAIL TO A PROFESSOR

A Listen to Ken's plan about visiting a lab during his stay in the U.S. and answer the following questions.

1. What is the name of the laboratory that Ken wants to visit?

2. How did Ken learn about the laboratory?

3. What does Professor Brown emphasize?

4. When is Ken planning to visit the laboratory?

B Read Ken's email. The expressions for 1 to 4 are somewhat impolite. Replace them with more formal and polite expressions.

To: Professor Brown

From: Ken Nakamura

Subject: Request to visit your laboratory

Dear Professor Brown,

My name is Ken Nakamura, and I'm a first-year master's student at Osaka Tech University in Japan. Currently, I am studying abroad at Rocklin University for three weeks. The reason why I am writing this email to you today is that your research topic is closely related to my interest in connecting research and business. I am very interested in your research, and If possible, **1. I want to visit your lab** during my stay. **2. Why don't you be available** sometime between August 10th and 17th? If you are too busy to meet me, **3. I will just meet your students** to receive a tour of your lab. I have attached a presentation of my research to this message.
4. Please reply to this email.

Sincerely,
Ken Nakamura

---

1. I want to visit your lab
   (a) I would like to visit your lab
   (b) let me visit your lab
   (c) allow me to visit your lab

2. Why don't you be available
   (a) Please be available
   (b) Would you be available
   (c) I want you to be available

3. I will just meet your students
   (a) I want to meet your students
   (b) I am happy to meet your students
   (c) I should meet your students

4. Please reply to this email.
   (a) I am impatiently waiting for your reply.
   (b) I am looking forward to hearing from you.
   (c) Contact me soon.

Read Ken's email again from B **and choose the correct answer.**

1. How many days will Ken be available to meet the professor?
   (a) for about a week
   (b) for about a month
   (c) he doesn't know yet

2. Why does Ken want to visit the lab?
   (a) His research is related to the professor's.
   (b) He wants to do his research at the lab.
   (c) The professor is the most famous in Ken's research field.

3. What does Ken propose in the case that the professor is busy?
   (a) He can tour the lab alone after receiving instructions from the lab students.
   (b) He can meet the professor's students for a tour.
   (c) He can talk with a lab student or the professor on the phone.

D **The following sentences are direct and, therefore, can be considered rude and informal. Change them into indirect questions.**

Ex.) When does the experiment start?	May I ask <u>when the experiment starts?</u>
1. How much does the program cost?	Would you mind telling me _____
2. Tell me if I need to take the examination.	Please let me know _____
3. What is your availability?	Could I know _____
4. How many students are in your lab?	Could you tell me _____
5. Where's the professor's office?	Do you know _____
6. Which textbook will we use?	Would you kindly tell me _____

PREPARATION FOR THE LAB VISIT
ENERGY AND TEMPERATURE

Ken received a reply from Professor Brown! Unfortunately, he'll be on a business trip during Ken's stay, but he suggested that Ken visit the laboratory and meet one of his students. Before visiting the lab, Ken decided to review the basics of energy and temperature by himself.

 Energy comes in various forms. Here are nine common types of energy. Fill in the blanks using words in the box.

| Radiant | Nuclear | Gravitational | Chemical | Mechanical |
| Electrical | Thermal | Elastic | | |

Energy: what makes matter move or change	
Energy type I	Energy type II
1._____ energy The energy that comes from the motion of an object or substance from one location to another.	5._____ energy The energy stored in the bonds of atoms and molecules resulting from chemical reactions that hold atoms or molecules together.
2._____ energy The energy from the movement of electrons in one direction, causing an electrical charge.	6._____ energy The energy that is caused by changes in the atomic nuclei.
3._____ energy The internal energy of something that comes from vibrations or movements of molecules.	7._____ energy The energy that an object has due to gravity because it is higher up above the ground. Bringing the object higher builds this energy up, and letting it fall uses it.
4._____ energy Light energy that is electromagnetic energy traveling in transverse waves.	8._____ energy The energy stored in an object due to it being stretched or compressed.
Sound energy The energy from vibrations that are transferred through air in a wave to produce audio.	

B Read the description of two different types of energy. Choose the correct category for Energy type I and Energy type II from **A** .

There are two types of energy: kinetic and potential.

Kinetic energy comes from objects that are moving. Take an airplane, for example, which has a significant amount of energy while flying in the air due to its fast velocity. Also, dropping an object off of a building, or a planet rotating around a sun are both examples of kinetic energy because they receive their energy from movement.

Potential energy is the energy an object has due to factors such as its position compared to another object, stresses within itself, and more. If you stand on top of a hill, for example, you have higher potential energy than standing at the bottom. Due to the forces of gravity, climbing up the hill is much more difficult than running down it, right? Potential energy is built up while you climb the hill and expended when you run down it.

1. Energy type I : _____ energy

2. Energy type II : _____ energy

PREPARATION FOR THE LAB VISIT
KINETIC ENERGY

Ken also studied various ways to generate electricity through kinetic energy. A power plant is an important example of kinetic energy transformation.

Match the vocabulary with the definitions.

1. hydroelectric power _____   (a) a machine that changes one type of energy into another, usually mechanical energy into electrical energy

2. turbine _____   (b) an oily, thick, and flammable substance that occurs naturally and is used in fuels like gasoline

3. generator _____   (c) a machine that generates power when things like water, steam, gas, air, etc. flow through its rotors

4. nuclear reactor _____   (d) something that allows fissile material to undergo a controlled, self-sustaining nuclear reaction that releases energy

5. radiation _____   (e) the generation and distribution of electricity created from the energy of falling or flowing water

6. geothermal power _____   (f) the process in which energy is emitted as particles or waves from one thing to another

7. fossil fuels _____   (g) using the internal heat of the Earth to create power

8. petroleum _____   (h) combustible organic material such as oil, coal, or natural gas that comes from the remains of living things

 Read the sentences about various ways to generate electricity and circle the correct words.

(a)	Wind stations transform wind energy into another useful kind of energy. A wind farm may **1.** (consisting / consist / consistency) of around a hundred wind turbines connected to an electric power **2.** (transmissible / transmission / transmutation) network.
(b)	Hydroelectric power plants are stations where energy is produced by the force of falling water. The water moves turbines, **3.** (generating / generated / generate) electricity that is collected in generators.
(c)	Heat is produced by fission in a nuclear reactor. This creates steam from the heated water. The pressurized steam is then pushed into a steam turbine.
(d)	Certain power plants create energy by transforming heat and light from the Sun. Two types of energies are produced. Solar thermal energy is stored from the heat of the Sun that **4.** (transformer / transformation / transforms) water into steam, moving turbines that are connected to a generator that collects energy. The other is photovoltaic energy. This is a **5.** (methodical / method / methodize) of generating electrical power by converting solar radiation into direct electric current.

(e)	Geothermal electricity is electricity **6.** (generated / generative / generic) from Earth's heat. Technologies that utilize this heat include dry steam, flash steam, and binary cycle power plants.
(f)	Coal-fired thermal power plants generate electrical energy from thermal energy. Since heat is generated by burning fossil fuels like coal, petroleum, or natural gasses, these are also collectively **7.** (referring / referred / referrer) to as the fossil-fueled power plants. Coal power plants were the earliest of the fossil fuel power plants to be built.

 C Match the pictures below with the explanations about generating electricity from **B**.

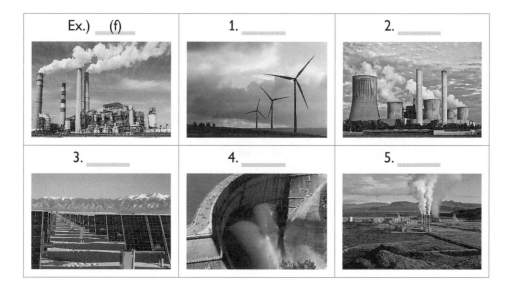

Ex.) (f)	1. _____	2. _____
3. _____	4. _____	5. _____

 D Read the explanation and choose the appropriate words from the box to label the picture.

Heat transfer is the process of transferring heat from a high-temperature reservoir to a low-temperature reservoir. It is the movement of heat across two different locations that have a temperature difference. This difference in temperature is called potential, and the flow of heat is called flux. There are three modes of heat transfer between two bodies.

Radiation is the heat transfer between two objects that are at different temperatures and are not directly touching each other, unlike conduction and convection, which require physical contact. Heat transfer occurs because of electromagnetic waves in the atmosphere. An example of this is the Sun heating up the Earth.

Conduction is the transfer of heat between two bodies that have different temperatures. The process occurs when two objects that are at different temperatures are put in direct contact with each other. For example: when one end of a metal object is heated, the heat will transfer all the way down to the other side.

Convection is the transfer of heat between a solid body and a liquid. An example of this is a pot of water being heated over a fire. Molecules in the water move rapidly because of the difference in temperature. Convection can even occur with gases, like what happens when you hear thunder.

Radiation	Conduction	Convection

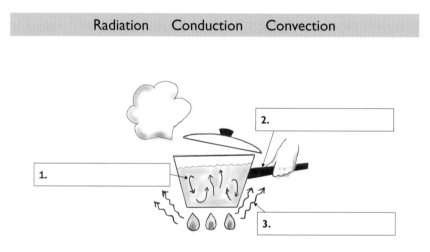

 Read each statement and choose the right answer.

Ex.) Rising warm air is an example of what?
  (a) radiation
  (b) conduction
  (c) convection

1. A thermometer works because its liquid contracts when heated. This is an example of what?

    (a) radiation

    (b) conduction

    (c) convection

2. As cool air touches a warm surface, the air begins to heat from what?

    (a) radiation

    (b) conduction

    (c) convection

3. This is the reason why water boils and creates a circular motion.

    (a) radiation

    (b) conduction

    (c) convection

4. This type of heat transfer takes place when you use a microwave to warm up a cup of tea.

    (a) radiation

    (b) conduction

    (c) convection

 Read the sentences and choose True or False.

1. The Sun directly heats the air in our atmosphere. [True / False]
2. Cool air rises while warm air sinks. [True / False]
3. A higher temperature means faster moving molecules. [True / False]
4. Black objects absorb more solar radiation than white objects. [True / False]

VISITING PROFESSOR BROWN'S LAB
MEETING A STUDENT

Ken will meet Kate, a Ph.D. student studying under Professor Brown. They will tour the laboratory together. Let's see how it goes.

Listen to the conversation while reading the dialog. Then choose similar meanings for the boldfaced words.

Ken : Nice to meet you. I'm Ken Nakamura. Please call me Ken. I'm very excited to visit Professor Brown's lab today.

Kate: Hi Ken, It's nice to meet you, too. My name's Kate. I'm a Ph.D. student at this lab and I'll be **1. in charge of** giving you a tour today.

Ken : Great, thank you so much. To be honest, Kate, I'm a little nervous.

Kate: Oh, don't worry, **2. you can take it easy**. Everyone here is very friendly and happy to have guests. Actually, I just came back from Osaka. I attended a conference there. Japan was amazing.

Ken : **3. No way!** I am from Osaka too.

Kate: Really? How interesting! I want to talk to you more about that later. But for now, **4. let's get started** on the tour. If you'd like, I'll first show you the main facilities.

Ken : **5. That sounds good**. Thank you again for taking time to do this for me today.

Kate: It's my pleasure. Please follow me.

1. in charge of
   (a) responsible for
   (b) collect the charge for
   (c) move fast in

2. you can take it easy
   (a) You can speak simple English.
   (b) You can be relaxed.
   (c) The tour will be easy.

3. No way!
   (a) Wow, really?
   (b) You cannot do that.
   (c) I got lost.

4. let's get started
   (a) let's finish our conversation
   (b) we have finished the start already
   (c) let's begin

5. That sounds good.
   (a) I hear an interesting sound.
   (b) I can agree with that.
   (c) I like that type of music.

Kate introduced the project of the Hoover Dam as an example of clean energy. After that, they had a discussion about renewable energy.

 B Answer the following questions with a partner.

1. What do you know about dams? How do you think they function?
2. Have you visited a dam before? If so, where was it? If not, would you like to?
3. What do you think the benefits of dams are?
4. What do you think the risks or disadvantages of dams are?

 C Read the sentences and choose the most appropriate words to replace the boldfaced words.

1. What is the **initial** step in constructing a dam?
   (a) first
   (b) last
   (c) most difficult

2. A hydroelectric dam **converts** potential energy into mechanical energy.
   (a) stops
   (b) renews
   (c) changes

3. Governments must **implement** clean energy legislation to protect the environment.
   (a) carry out
   (b) ignore
   (c) remember

4. Generating enough electricity to supply future demands **poses** a difficult challenge.
   (a) takes
   (b) presents
   (c) decreases

5. We must all **contribute to** society by cutting down on our electricity usage.
   (a) add value to
   (b) hold off on
   (c) withhold from

 Read the description of Hoover Dam's history. The paragraph order has been changed. Put the paragraphs in the correct order.

1st _____ ⟹ 2nd __(c)__ ⟹ 3rd _____ ⟹ 4th _____

(a) In the early 20ᵗʰ century, the U.S. Bureau of Reclamation created the initial plans for a massive dam on the Arizona-Nevada border to control the Colorado River. The proposed dam would provide several benefits. Hydroelectric power could be generated by converting fast-flowing water into mechanical energy. Additional benefits would include improved flood control, agricultural irrigation, and improved water supply.

(b) Hoover Dam is now a major sightseeing destination, with some seven million visitors a year, and nearly one million of them take the tour. It will continue to be known as one of the greatest engineering projects of the 20ᵗʰ century and a monument to the ingenuity of the nation's engineers and the power of its machines.

(c) Implementing the construction within the strict timeframe posed a great challenge, and workers drilled into carbon monoxide-filled tunnels and hung from heights of 800 feet to clear the canyon walls.

(d) Thanks to the effort of many engineers, Hoover Dam was completed in 1935 and became the world's largest dam at the time. It became a national historic landmark that contributes to storing enough water in Lake Mead to irrigate 2 million acres of land.

DISCUSSION   RENEWABLE ENERGY

 Read the discussion between Ken, Kate, and her lab mate Chris and change the underlined parts to the correct order.

Kate : Today, I'd like to talk about the recent Hoover Dam project proposal. As you may already know, Hoover Dam is one of the greatest engineering marvels in American history. But what you may not have heard is that, **1.** (to / recent / according / news), it may soon play an important role as a solution for storing renewable energy.

Ken : Actually, I think I also heard about this. I believe they were discussing a new solution for storing renewable energy in a way in which they can obtain more energy without causing environmental damage, right?

Kate : Yes, that's correct, Ken. Chris, have you also heard about this?

Chris : No, I haven't. However, it does seem interesting.

Ken : Actually, I only briefly read about it. I'm not sure about the details.

Kate : Well, what do you know about California's power situation?

Chris : **2.** (if / not / I / am / mistaken), California is in need of more power sources. They've been focusing on producing it through clean energy. However, despite being one of the sunniest states in the U.S., it has issues with utilizing the full potential of sources like solar and wind power.

Ken : Why's that?

Chris : One reason is that it's difficult to store the collected power when a lot is produced. Instead, California transfers the excess energy to other states and then burns fossil fuels again when there is no wind or sunshine.

Kate : Yes, Chris, that's correct.

Ken : I see. So that's where Hoover Dam comes in?

Kate : Exactly. **3.** (mentioning / was / as / I / before), there are plans underway for a $3 billion wind and solar-powered pump station near the dam. Water would be pumped from downstream and back up into Lake Mead where it originally started. Electricity can be regulated by releasing the water back through the dam when needed, acting like a giant battery. I think it's a great idea to help California achieve a sustainable source of electricity. But I want to hear how you feel about it.

Chris: That's a very unique approach, and I hope it can be realized. But it will cost a lot of money, and it's important to know who will pay for it. For example, will taxes need to be increased?

Ken : **4.** (what / say / to / going / was / I / exactly / that's). It would be great if they are able to afford it. However, California already has some of the highest taxes in the country.

Kate : **5.** (I / you / with / point / that / on / agree). It would be interesting to find out how the project will be funded. But if California doesn't put money towards generating sustainable energy, it may end up costing much more in the long run.

1. to / recent / according / news

2. if / not / I / am / mistaken

3. mentioning / was / as / I / before

4. what / say / to / going / was / I / exactly / that's

5. I / you / with / point / that / on / agree

B Answer the questions regarding the reading from *A*.

1. How can Hoover Dam play an important role in the near future?

2. What is the difficulty with using solar and wind energy in California?

3. What is Chris's concern regarding the project?

C Write your opinion about efforts towards clean energy in Japan by referring to *A* . Hint: Try using the useful expressions below.

According to (person/article), …
If I am not mistaken, …
As (person/article) mentioned before, …
I agree with (person/article) on that point.

After three weeks of rewarding experiences in the U.S., Ken is ready to return to Japan for a new adventure!

Computing and Future Technology

▌INTRODUCTION   ATTENDING A WORKSHOP

After coming back from studying abroad, Ken became very motivated and decided to join a workshop in English with John.

 Listen to the story about attending a workshop and answer the following questions.

1. Which workshop does Ken plan to attend?

    (a) a workshop about future energy

    (b) a workshop about sustainable energy

    (c) a workshop about future technology

2. When will the workshop be held?

    (a) August 30th (b) August 13th (c) August 15th

3. What is Ken's main purpose for attending the workshop?

    (a) to expand his social networking connections

    (b) to meet famous people

    (c) to improve his English

4. What is Ken's concern regarding the workshop?

    (a) He thinks his English is not good enough to communicate with other people.

    (b) He is worried that he doesn't have enough computer-related knowledge.

    (c) He is concerned about attending it alone.

B Make full sentences by using the phrases below. Look up examples online if needed.

Ex.) discuss with…

Ken discussed the renewable energy project with Kate.

1. happened to….

2. given the importance of….

3. make sure to….

C Discuss the following questions with a partner.

1. Have you joined a workshop before? If so, what kind of workshop was it?
2. Are you interested in attending a workshop about future technology? Why / why not?
3. What kind of workshop would you like to attend? Why?

D Before looking at the workshop registration form, try to figure out what these words mean. Draw lines to their definitions.

Ex.) indicate   (a) to explain something in a clear way

1. consent   (b) to not include something or someone

2. confirm   (c) to supply or give something

3. provide   (d) to agree to something

4. exclude   (e) to show something to someone

5. vary   (f) to be different from something else

6. specify   (g) to check and make sure that something is correct

Read Ken's registration form below and answer the questions.

REGISTRATION FORM

The 10th Workshop for Future Technology

Mirai Tech University, Tokyo, Japan

Please fill out this form electronically and submit to: workshop@futuretech.com

Registration Date   August 23rd, 20XX

Registration Details

• First Name: __Ken__ Last Name: __Nakamura__ / Email: knakamura@ot.ac.jp

• Affiliation: Graduate School of Engineering, Osaka Tech University / Position: Graduate Student

• ☐ I would like to request special accommodations for certain facilities.

     If so, please specify (wheelchair, hearing assistance, etc.) _____

Registration Fee [1,2]

	Members of FutureTech		Non-Members	
General Registration Fee	☐	$250	☐	$350
Reduced Registration Fee (Organizing members)	☐	$150	☐	$250
Students and Retired Delegates	☑	$100	☐	$120

[1] The registration fee includes the workshop materials and dinner reception but excludes personal expenses such as transportation and lodging.

[2] Complete the registration and payment by August 24th to receive a $20 early bird discount taken off the full price at the payment page.

Become a FutureTech member when registering for this workshop and receive the discounted member rate!

☑ I confirm that I would like to become a member of FutureTech to take advantage of the discounted price.

*If you checked the box above, indicate if you are registering as an individual or corporation.

☑ Individual FutureTech member   ☐ corporate FutureTech member

Cancellation Policy & Other Information

• Cancellations received on or before August 24th are subject to a charge of 10% of the registration fees. No refunds will be provided for cancellations after August 24th. Admission is transferable at no extra cost as long as both parties consent. Please notify the organizers beforehand if you cannot attend and indicate the name of the individual who will attend instead.

• Availability of lodging and plane tickets may vary depending on the number of attendees. Please plan accordingly.

☑ FutureTech would like to occasionally keep you informed of our events and other related information. If you do not desire this, please check this box to be removed from our general distribution list.

1. How much is the registration fee for Ken if he pays before Aug. 24th?
   (a) $80
   (b) $100
   (c) $120

2. Did Ken sign up to receive updated information from FutureTech?
   (a) No, he chose not to be informed.
   (b) Yes, he chose to receive information from FutureTech.
   (c) We don't know.

3. If Ken cancels the registration on Aug. 24th, how much of a fee would he have to pay?
   (a) $8
   (b) $100
   (c) $80

4. What does the registration fee include?
   (a) the materials for the workshop
   (b) the materials for the workshop and dinner reception
   (c) the materials for the workshop, transportation, lodging, and dinner reception

5. If Ken cannot go to the workshop, can his lab mate join instead?
   (a) No, there are no transfers once the ticket has been purchased.
   (b) Yes, as long as Ken indicates who will be going instead.
   (c) Yes. Ken only needs to give his lab mate the ticket.

PREPARING FOR THE WORKSHOP

To prepare for the workshop, Ken decided to study the basics of computing and future technology in advance.

 The pictures below represent the functions of a computer. Choose the right word for each picture.

~~input and output~~	finding	securing	storing
counting	sorting	processing	calculating	communicating

Ex.) input and output	**1.** _____	**2.** _____
	1, 2, 3...	
3. _____	**4.** _____	**5.** _____
6. _____	**7.** _____	**8.** _____
1 + 2 = 3 2 + 2 = 4	BIN Burnable Non Burnable	

Read the explanation about hardware and software and answer the questions in complete sentences.

Hardware is any physical device that is used in machines. By physical, we mean that you can touch it. This includes such things as monitors, keyboards, and mice. Hardware can also be the components inside a computer like the hard drive and motherboard. Hardware acts as the physical body of a machine, and its role is to be the delivery system for software.

Software, on the other hand, is not physical and instead consists of only executable code. Examples of software include a computer's operating system, a downloaded app on a cellphone, or an internet browser. Each has code that runs in order to accomplish a task. In this regard, software acts as the brain of a machine.

The relationship between hardware and software is that they are interdependent, meaning they both need each other to function properly. Software gives commands to hardware regarding tasks that need to be performed, and hardware executes these tasks. Therefore, they are both necessary for many devices ranging from laptop computers to cellphones, satellites, and airplanes. Since hardware is physical, it is more difficult to switch out the components compared to software; software can simply receive updated code commands.

Finally, you may have heard of a firewall before, which is a tool used to monitor and protect ingoing and outgoing internet activity. Most people affiliate firewalls with software due to them being more common. However, hardware firewalls also exist and are typically found in broadband routers.

1. What part of the body does hardware represent?

2. What part of the body does software represent?

3. What is the connection between hardware and software?

4. What is the purpose of a firewall?

Divide the items into two groups between software and hardware.

Ex.) spyware

1. a robotic arm   • software

2. a mouse

3. a modem

4. a computer virus

5. a mainframe computer   • hardware

6. an electronic database

7. an operating system

 Look at the three pictures and answer True or False.

Picture #1	Picture #2	Picture #3		
The internet in this room is fast	Internet	Name	Grade	Department
		John	4	Literature
		Ryan	3	Law
		Kathy	1	Engineering

1. The text box in Picture #1 is borderless. [True / False]
2. The text in Picture #2 has been rotated 60 degrees clockwise. [True / False]
3. The text and background colors in the top bar have been reversed in Picture #3.

                                             [True / False]

4. All of the cells are the same size in Picture #3. [True / False]
5. There are four columns and three rows in Picture #3. [True / False]
6. The middle column has a light shade in Picture #3. [True / False]
7. The table gridlines are grey in Picture #3. [True / False]
8. The text is centered within the cells in Picture #3. [True / False]

Write the punctuation marks or symbols for the word/s.

Word/s	Symbol
Ex.) arrow	→
1. exclamation mark	
2. hash symbol	
3. hyphen	
4. asterisk	
5. comma	
6. "at" sign	
7. forward slash	
8. quotation marks	
9. parentheses	

 Match the words on the left with the words on the right.

Ex.) arrange the ___(d)___	(a) new window
1. cut and paste _____	(b) a program
2. install _____	(c) some text
3. open the document in a _____	(d) icons on the desktop
4. copy _____	(a) for a lost file
5. launch _____	(b) an application
6. search _____	(c) some text
7. send the file _____	(d) to a different folder
8. accidentally delete an _____	(a) program
9. exit a _____	(b) important file
10. click _____	(c) as a web page
11. view _____	(d) on the taskbar
12. close down an _____	(a) after saving a document
13. log off _____	(b) application
14. put the file _____	(c) hard drive
15. wipe the _____	(d) on a USB memory drive

68

DISCUSSION
ARTIFICIAL INTELLIGENCE PREDICTIONS

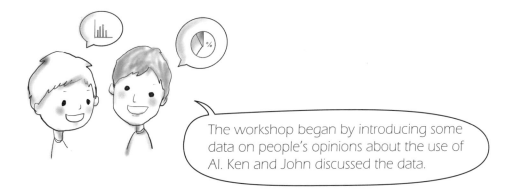

The workshop began by introducing some data on people's opinions about the use of AI. Ken and John discussed the data.

 Answer the following questions with a partner.

1. What do you know about Artificial Intelligence (AI)?

_____

2. What's a product that can benefit from using AI? Why?

_____

3. What is the biggest benefit that AI can provide in the future? Why?

_____

4. Do you think AI is dangerous? What are the risks of AI?

_____

 Listen to the sentences and write the word for each blank. Some words need to be modified. Then listen again and shadow the audio.

implication   justify   diminish   precise   exceed

1. There are some who predict that AI will cause people's intelligence to _____ .
2. On the other hand, others think that the utilization of AI is _____ .
3. Those that think that they don't need AI for recruiting purposes at all _____ half of the participants.

4. The AI systems were _____ more than 80% of the time.
5. Many people are debating the _____ of relying on AI, as it continues to rapidly exceed our expectations.

  C Listen to the explanation of the graph regarding what people think about AI. Complete the graph by writing the percentage.

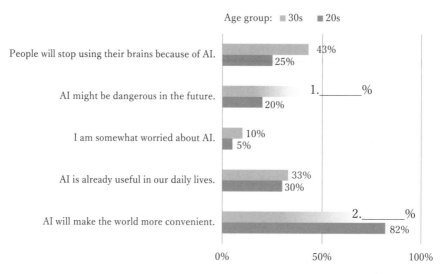

Age group: ■ 30s ■ 20s

People will stop using their brains because of AI. — 43% / 25%

AI might be dangerous in the future. — 1._____% / 20%

I am somewhat worried about AI. — 10% / 5%

AI is already useful in our daily lives. — 33% / 30%

AI will make the world more convenient. — 2._____% / 82%

0%   50%   100%

WHAT DO YOU THINK ABOUT AI?

  D Listen to the next part and write the correct percentages.

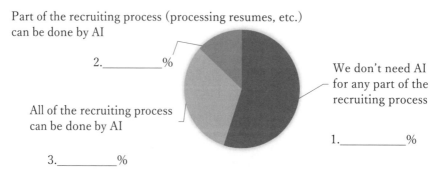

Part of the recruiting process (processing resumes, etc.) can be done by AI
2._____%

We don't need AI for any part of the recruiting process
1._____%

All of the recruiting process can be done by AI
3._____%

IF AI WAS IN CHARGE OF THE RECRUITING PROCESS, HOW WOULD YOU FEEL ABOUT IT?

E Listen to the next part and write the correct percentage or word.

Jobs that will be taken over		Jobs that won't be taken over	
Phone operator	99%	Doctor	0.4%
Data inputter	1. _____ %	Teacher	0.4%
Cashier	97%	Writer	4%
Taxi driver	2. _____ %	3. _____	4.2%
Manufacturer	80%	Artist	5%

PRESENTATION
ARTIFICIAL INTELLIGENCE PREDICTIONS

One of the presenters will give a speech about AI. Let's practice some useful expressions beforehand to give a presentation.

First, unscramble the sentences in the correct order. Then check your answers by listening to the audio.

1. appreciate / this opportunity / to / I / present / my research
   _____ to you today.

2. going / I / am / to give / regarding / a presentation / the topic of
   _____ "What will

   our future be like with AI?".

3. me / let / outlining / begin by
   Now, _____ my presentation.

4. begin / I / will / by / providing / on / background information
   _____ AI.

5. will / introduce / I / opinions / two opposite
   Then _____ .

6. finally, / I / how / describe / will
   _____ the future world would be like with AI.

7. me / summarize / let /my
   Now, _____ presentation.

8. would / to / like / I / emphasize / that
   _____ there are two opposite sides to the debate.

Now, read the presenter's script and answer True or False.

I appreciate this opportunity to present my research to you. My name is Ryan White from Auburn University, and today I am going to give a presentation regarding the topic of "What will our future be like with AI?".

Before starting my presentation, I want you to imagine a future where AI is everywhere in our daily lives. Does this make you feel happy? Or are there any concerns? I want you to keep these questions in mind throughout this presentation. Now, let me first outline my presentation. I will begin by providing background information on AI. Then I will introduce two opposite opinions of CEOs of IT companies in Silicon Valley. Finally, I will describe how the future world would be like with AI.

So, let's begin with some background information on AI.

[…]

I'll now discuss the opposing views about AI. With the recent rapid increase in the use of AI, both optimistic and pessimistic feelings for the future have been created. As AI continues to exceed our expectations, debates have been created regarding its implications. Famous CEOs from Silicon Valley IT companies are now stepping into the debate.

Last year, Tesla and SpaceX CEO Elon Musk cautioned against the potential negative consequences of AI. Musk stated that robots "will be able to do everything better than us," and that AI poses a threat to our safety and well-being because the number of people's jobs may diminish.

However, Facebook CEO Mark Zuckerberg opposed this argument, arguing that the use of AI, technology is justified. He stated, "I think you can build things, and the world gets better. But with AI, especially, I am really optimistic … AI is going to deliver so many improvements in the quality of our lives."

Now, let me summarize my presentation. The use of AI has the potential to make our lives better, but it also has various dangers. I would like to emphasize that there are still two opposite debates right now instead of a single agreement. And as AI continues to advance, it will surely remain an issue worth debating.

Thank you for your time. I'll be happy to answer any questions you have.

Source: https://www.businessinsider.sg/mark-zuckerberg-said-elon-musks-doomsday-ai-predictions-are-irresponsible-2017-7/

1. Zuckerberg thinks that we should slow down our use of AI. [True / False]
2. Zuckerberg is positive about utilizing AI in our daily lives. [True / False]
3. Musk believes people may lose their jobs in the future due to AI. [True / False]
4. Musk is more optimistic than Zuckerberg about the potential of AI. [True / False]

C Write your opinion for each question in full sentences. Then discuss the questions with a partner.

1. What are the dangers of AI?

2. How is AI helping us today?

3. How intelligent will AI become?

4. What are the differences between AI and human intelligence?

Ken and John really enjoyed the workshop!

Student Club Activities

Measurements and Mechanisms

INTRODUCTION
THE BACKGROUND OF A COMPETITION

Ken is going to enter a competition!

$\boxed{A}$ Listen to the dialog while reading and filling in the blanks.

In this unit, Ken, John and their classmate Lin will learn about an upcoming engineering competition where **1.**_____ _____ _____ universities will participate in constructing and piloting an aircraft that can fly the farthest. After reading the details, they'll become interested in competing. However, to achieve such a task, they must first learn about the **2.**_____ of measurements and mechanisms; accurate measurements are required to construct a flying device, and various mechanisms are involved in operating it. Ken also needs to be able to cooperate with his partners using English and therefore needs to be able to use **3.**_____ expressions and vocabulary while communicating with each other. You may **4.**_____ this type of opportunity in your life as well, so **5.**_____ _____ and **6.**_____ _____ what happens!

B Below are some parts from A. Choose the same meaning as the boldfaced words.

1. **find out** what happens
   - (a) discover what happens
   - (b) think about what happens
   - (c) try to select what happens

2. the **aspects of** measurements
   - (a) the positive measurements
   - (b) the parts of measurements
   - (c) the originality of measurements

3. **pay attention**
   - (a) take notice
   - (b) ignore everything
   - (c) settle down

4. you may **encounter** this opportunity
   - (a) suffer from this opportunity
   - (b) lose this opportunity
   - (c) experience this opportunity

5. use **relevant** expressions
   - (a) use important expressions
   - (b) use improper expressions
   - (c) use appropriate expressions

6. **a number of** universities
   - (a) several universities
   - (b) unknown universities
   - (c) only a couple of universities

C Complete the sentences by choosing the most appropriate words or expressions. Use each word or expression only one time.

| a number of | relevant | encountered |
| pay attention | come up with | |

To be able to **1.**_____ plans for constructing an aircraft, one must understand both measurements and mechanisms. First, measurements are important for designing and constructing the base aircraft. We take measurements to figure out the dimensions, or size, of different parts. Here, it is important to **2.**_____ to accuracy to make sure the plane is balanced and durable to avoid crashing! Next are the mechanisms, which are the aircraft's moving parts. Mechanisms do things like turn wheels and cranks and spin rotors and gears. There are, of course, **3.**_____ aircraft that have no mechanisms. They are made out of rigid materials that don't move. You may have **4.**_____ these as a child if you've ever made a paper airplane. Instead of propelling themselves in the air, they rely on wind to fly. However, paper airplanes are not **5.**_____ to Ken's group's aircraft, as theirs will involve complex mechanisms.

AN ADVERTISEMENT FOR AN ENGINEERING COMPLETION

> Ken found a brochure advertising a flying competition. Let's see what it's about!

 Read each sentence and choose the letter that best replaces the boldfaced words.

1. Contestants will be judged on their ability to **differentiate** their team from the rest.
   (a) show the similarities of
   (b) show the uniqueness of
   (c) show their confidence of

2. You must **demonstrate** that you are in good physical condition through an exercise test.
   (a) hide
   (b) show
   (c) be careful

3. Contestants must have an **adequate** ability to swim to qualify. Those with an **inadequate** ability to pass the swimming test cannot participate.
   (a) acceptable, unacceptable
   (b) pleasant, unpleasant
   (c) unique, equal

4. Let's **convene** at Lake Biwa. Please call me when you arrive.
   (a) confirm
   (b) separate
   (c) gather together

5. What are the selection **criteria** for the aircraft materials?
   (a) quality
   (b) guesses
   (c) principles

 Read the advertisement and answer the questions.

UNIVERSITY FLYING COMPETITION

The Shiga local government is happy to announce the 10th annual University Flying Competition! Contestants will design and construct their own aircraft and launch them off a giant ramp to fly over (or crash into) the lake. This year, we'll be convening at Lake Biwa on November 2nd, where the event will last all day from 7:00 – 16:00.

Contestants will be judged on three criteria: airtime (how long the plane flies), flight distance (how far the plane travels), and creative design by demonstrating the capacity to differentiate one's team from the rest. Prizes will be awarded in the form of scholarships to those who place in first, second, or third. Nevertheless, all contestants will receive a certificate of participation.

Students from all universities can participate, and there is no set limit for the number of applicants. There is also no application fee, and those who wish to only spectate at the event can do so free of charge. However, the event committee members will select just 30 teams to take part in the main event. Applicants who are selected to compete must pay the standard entry fee, as well as demonstrate an adequate ability to swim and be in good physical condition. Those with serious health conditions or an inadequate ability to pass a swimming test are therefore kindly asked to refrain from applying. For additional information, visit our website and select 'Event Rules and Safety.'

Please note that the event will be held rain or shine, but may be canceled in the event of extreme weather. Please sign up for our email mailing list to receive updates and notifications of potential cancellations.

We are looking forward to seeing you there!

Ex.) How many teams are competing? <u>There will be 30 teams selected to compete.</u>

1. Where and when will the event be held? _____

2. How will the contestants be judged? _____

3. Is the event free for spectators? _____

4. What are the requirements to participate as a competitor? _____

_____

5. Where can people find more information about the event? _____

_____

> Ken is discussing the competition with Lin, his classmate. Ken, Lin, and John will form a team to compete.

 C First, listen to the dialog while taking notes. Then answer the following questions with a partner.

1. What are the classmates discussing?
2. What did they say the benefits are for participating?
3. Do you think the group will participate? Why?/why not?
4. Has Lin already agreed to join?
5. Does this event seem interesting to you? Why/why not?

The group is communicating through instant messaging. Read each message and choose its main purpose from the options in the box.

(a) requesting a response to an unanswered question
(b) asking for clarification
(c) scheduling a time to meet
(d) making a correction

1. _____

John

Hey guys. As you know, the deadline is approaching soon. I'm not entirely sure about how much more time is required to complete everything, and it seems like we still need to finish early enough to have adequate time to run tests. If you could let me know when's a good time for everyone to convene to discuss this further, that'd be great. Thanks.

sent at 11:00

2. _____

Lin

Ken, there was something that I wanted to go over regarding the document you recently sent me. You know, the one about our selection criteria for the aircraft materials. Are you saying that we should purchase the most expensive materials, or is medium grade fine? Sorry, but I just need this to be clearly explained since we can't return the materials once we purchase them. Let me know. Thanks.

sent at 12:31

3. _____

Ken

There's been a slight change of plans regarding the workflow schedule that I recently sent everyone. I just realized that I'm busy this weekend, so I'm actually not going to be able to finish my work by the time that I stated. I'll have to finish it early next week. I've updated the information and resent the document. Please disregard the previous one.

sent at 1:03

4. _____

Ken

Hi guys. I want to follow up on the question I asked previously since no one responded yet. I kind of need an answer soon. If you don't mind, could you let me know your availability next week?

sent at 12:25

DOING THE MEASUREMENTS I
DRAWING UP THE BLUEPRINTS

The group is reviewing the basics of measurements.

 First, look at the pictures and write the appropriate names in the blanks. Then match the instruments with the parameters they measure.

| stopwatch | tape measure | thermometer | multimeter | scale |

(a) _____   (b) _____   (c) _____   (d) _____   (e) _____

1. This measures the parameter of time.   (a) (b) (c) (d) (e)
2. This measures electrical currents.   (a) (b) (c) (d) (e)
3. This measures the parameter of mass.   (a) (b) (c) (d) (e)
4. This measures the parameter of length.   (a) (b) (c) (d) (e)
5. This measures the parameter of temperature.   (a) (b) (c) (d) (e)

Height, length, and width are all dimensions.
Dimensions are the measurements of objects.

B Read each description and write the proper aircraft parameter from the picture.

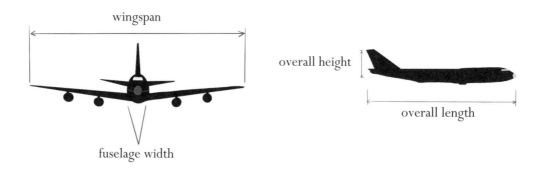

1. This is a measurement of the dimensions for how tall the aircraft is from the wheels, all the way up to the top of the aircraft's tail. _____
2. This is a measurement of the dimensions for how wide the aircraft is. The wings are the widest part of the plane, so we measure how far they reach. _____
3. This is a measurement of the dimensions for how long the plane is. The measurement is taken from the nose of the plane, all the way to the tail.

    _____
4. This is a measurement of the dimensions for how wide the main body of the plane is, excluding the wings. _____

Listen to the explanation of the dimensions of an aircraft's fuselage and choose the appropriate word. Not all words are used.

cross section	circumference	radius	diameter	arc

4.

2.

1.

3.

 Complete the sentences by matching the words with their description.

Ex.) A fuselage is … ——————— (a) the main body of an aircraft.

1. The circumference is …

2. The radius is …

3. The diameter is …

4. A cross section is …

5. An arc is …

(b) a line from the center of a circle to the outside section.

(c) a line from one side of a circle that passes through the center, reaching the opposite end.

(d) the measurement around an entire circle.

(e) a section of a circle that bends in a curved angle.

(f) something that has been cut open to be visualized as a flat surface.

WORKING TOGETHER TO PLAN THE PROJECT

The group is working hard to plan the project.

 Read the safety event rules and answer the questions.

Event Rules and Safety:

Paragraph 1 The following includes a list of items that contestants must have with them at the time of the competition. First, all contestants must bring their own life jackets and helmets, and this gear must be worn at all times when piloting the aircraft or standing on the launch pad. [...]

Paragraph 2 To ensure everyone's safety, the following precautions must be taken. Pilots cannot be strapped into the plane or enclosed in a capsule; they must ride on top of the aircraft. Contestants are advised to design their aircraft accordingly, while still making sure that the pilot will not be in danger of falling off the runway during launching. All members must be able to swim 40 meters unaided, and a swimming test will be administered prior to the event to which participation is mandatory. Contestants are not allowed to drink alcohol on the day of the event or the prior day. [...]

Paragraph 3 For specific dimensions of the aircraft, please click this link. In general, the aircraft can be no more than 2.5 meters in length and cannot exceed 300 kg in weight. Keep in mind that designs are subject to safety inspections, and adjustments may have to be made according to the safety team's discretion. [...]

Paragraph 4 It is important that each contestant reads and understands these rules. Everyone will be required to sign and confirm his or her compliance in this regard. Those who do not comply with these rules will be disqualified from the event. Please contact the event coordinator if you have questions or concerns. [...]

1. Which paragraph explains the requirements for the aircraft design and contestants' physical condition?   (1, 2, 3, 4)
2. Which paragraph addresses the consequences of not following the rules?
                                                                            (1, 2, 3, 4)
3. Which paragraph talks about the necessary equipment?   (1, 2, 3, 4)
4. Which paragraph talks about the aircrafts' measurement criteria?   (1, 2, 3, 4)

 Circle True or False regarding the Rules and Safety from **.**

1. Helmets and life jackets must be worn while piloting the aircraft. [True / False]
2. Pilots must be sealed inside the aircraft. [True / False]
3. An aircraft measuring 2.5 meters in length and 200 kg in weight will automatically be accepted. [True / False]
4. Taking part in the swimming test is recommended, but optional. [True / False]

C **Listen to the conversation and mark ✕ if the task is not required. If the task is required, write ○ and the required completion date.**

Tasks to complete	✕ / ○	Due date for completion
Ex.) Draw up blueprints	○	September 4th
1. Submit a rough draft to the professor		
2. Complete the measurements		
3. Acquire the materials		
4. Get a second opinion		
5. Finish the assembly		
6. Finish test flights		

DOING THE MEASUREMENTS II **ACCURACY**

A Read the following explanation about accuracy and match the vocabulary in the box with the correct description.

Measuring the dimensions of an aircraft can be quite difficult, as there are many pieces involved with complicated shapes and sizes. Being precise is important because both the aircraft's weight and size must be perfectly balanced to ensure that it can fly accurately. There are several technical words that are important to determine if an aircraft is built precisely or imprecisely. For example, clearance measures how much space an object has without hitting another object. And, while precision is important, measurements do not always have to be 100% accurate every time. Sometimes we allow a little room for error, which is known as tolerance. If an object has been measured within an acceptable amount of accuracy, we say that it is within tolerance. Furthermore, if something has met all measurement requirements and is within tolerance, we can say that it is permissible and can accept it. Otherwise, we reject it.

1. An object that can be accepted is ___.	(a) imprecise
2. A measurement that is not accurate is ___.	(b) clearance
3. The amount of extra space between objects is called ___.	(c) permissible

4. When something is measured correctly, it is ___.	(d) tolerance
5. The area of acceptance is known as ___.	(e) reject
6. Not accepting something means to ___ it.	(f) precise

Read each sentence and decide whether to accept or reject the item. Write O to accept items or ✕ to reject them.

	Within tolerance - Accept it [O]	Not within tolerance - Reject it [✕]
Ex.) These measurements are precise.	O	
1. This was cut accurately.		
2. The measurements are permissible.		
3. The measurements are inaccurate.		
4. There is adequate clearance.		
5. The amount of clearance is more than tolerable.		
6. These measurements are imprecise.		

LEARNING ABOUT MECHANISMS

 Read about components, mechanisms, and assemblies and answer the questions.

A component is one piece of a whole system. To better understand this, imagine a finished product such as a television. It has many small parts inside, right? These parts are considered the television's components. When several components are fitted together, they create useful functions such as a switch that turns the TV on or off or changes its channels. These collections of several components to create functioning things are called mechanisms. In other words, mechanisms are made up of components. Finally, an assembly is a whole unit consisting of various mechanisms. Notice that the word 'assembly' has 'assemble' in it. Assemble means to put things together. Therefore, an assembly is any whole thing that has been constructed from mechanisms. For example, a car's headlight is an assembly. This assembly has mechanisms inside it, and these mechanisms are made up of various components.

1. An example of a component is…	(a) a screw in a wristwatch (b) a television (c) a chair
2. An example of a mechanism is…	(a) a block of wood (b) a gear-shifter on a bike (c) a screw in a wristwatch
3. An example of an assembly is…	(a) a sheet of metal (b) an engine in a car (c) a long, solid pole

Let's look at some common mechanisms!

  Listen to the explanation for each mechanism and select the letter with the type of mechanism that is being described.

1. gear mechanism (a b c)   2. pulley mechanism (a b c)   3. crank mechanism (a b c)

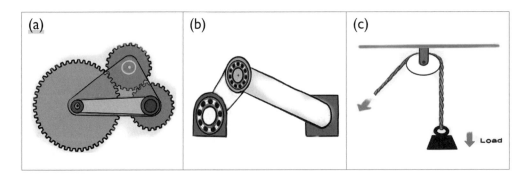

$\mathcal{C}$ Look at the pictures of other mechanisms. Discuss with a partner how each mechanism functions and what it can be used for.

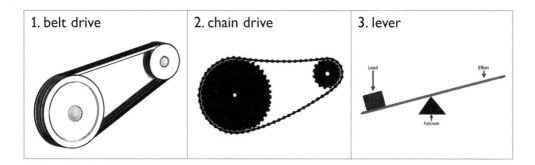

1. belt drive	2. chain drive	3. lever

$\mathcal{D}$ Work with a partner. Take turns having one person secretly choose one of the mechanism pictures from $\mathcal{B}$ or $\mathcal{C}$. Describe the mechanism and have the other person guess the correct one.

COMPETING IN THE EVENT

The day of the competition finally came! Let's see how it went!

Learn some useful expressions before listening to the conclusion. Choose the closest meaning to the sentence while paying attention to the boldfaced expressions.

1. Not everything **worked out** exactly as planned.
   (a) The beginning was difficult, but the result was good.
   (b) We exercised less than we had expected to.
   (c) The result was not the same as we thought it was going to be.

2. John **gave me a hand** with preparing lunch.
   (a) John gave me lunch.
   (b) I helped John with making lunch.
   (c) John helped me make lunch.

3. **It turns out** that we didn't do so well.
   (a) The conclusion was that we didn't do so well.
   (b) We changed our direction.
   (c) We didn't do well from the beginning.

4. We **shouldn't have cut** so many **corners**!
   (a) It was bad that we spent too much time doing things.
   (b) It was bad that we skipped steps.
   (c) It was bad that we went too fast.

5. We **missed the mark** by a lot!
   (a) We did not even come close to succeeding.
   (b) We forgot to think about what's important.
   (c) We got tired of doing the project.

B Listen to the outcome of the competition and choose the correct sequence of events.

C Answer the following questions with a partner.

1. What do you think the group should have done to make their aircraft fly more successfully?
2. Have you competed in an event before? Describe it.
3. What type of project would you both like to work on together? Why?

The team had a great time competing in the event!

Touring a Shipyard

Fluid and Air Dynamics

Ken will join a class that will tour a shipyard.

INTRODUCTION **TAKING A CLASS**

 Listen to the audio and answer the following questions.

1. Why did Ken decide to take the course on ocean engineering?
   (a) His major requires him to complete it.
   (b) He wants to widen his viewpoint and knowledge of Engineering.
   (c) Lin suggested that he take the course.

2. Why will Ken visit a shipyard?
   (a) Lin invited him to go since he has never seen one before.
   (b) He is interested in the process of shipbuilding.
   (c) The class will tour it as part of the course he is taking.

3. Choose the sentence that is INCORRECT regarding Lin.
   (a) Lin is a friend with the same major as Ken.
   (b) Lin is a friend who is attending the same class as Ken.
   (c) Lin is an international student who helps Ken.

4. What information is NOT mentioned in this listening?
   (a) what Lin's major is
   (b) the name of the course that Ken will take
   (c) the process of shipbuilding

B Listen to the professor explain the background of the tour to the class and circle True or False for each statement.

1. The objective of the tour is to study theories in fluid and air dynamics.
   [True / False]
2. Only some of Seto Shipbuilding Company's shipyards face the Seto Inland Sea.
   [True / False]
3. Seto Shipbuilding Company has a European office in Amsterdam.
   [True / False]
4. The shipyard that the class will visit is responsible for research and development.
   [True / False]
5. The shipyard builds one particular type of ship.
   [True / False]

 C Listen to the explanation again and fill in the blanks.

Professor:

We have studied the basic mechanisms and structures of ships so far. Now, while it is important for students to study theories in fluid and air dynamics in the classroom, it is also essential to learn how to **1.** _____ _____ _____ _____ _____.
It is **2.** _____ _____ _____ that we will be touring a ship manufacturing company.

Seto Shipbuilding Company has several shipyards, all of which face the Seto Inland Sea. One is located in Hiroshima and the others in Ehime. The company also has an office in Tokyo, as well as a European office in Amsterdam. The shipyard that we will visit next week is the newest one and is **3.** _____ _____ _____ the research and development of new technologies for the company. It has three dry docks, one of which is the largest in the company. The shipyard builds a large line-up of ships of all different sizes for various purposes.

PREPARING FOR THE TOUR   SAFETY TIPS

 Listen to the instructions and circle (O) the things that are permissible. Cross out (X) the things that are not allowed.

Ex.)	1.	2.	3.	4.
	5.	6.	7.	8.

B Answer the following questions based on *A*.

1. Why do visitors need to wear long-sleeved shirts?

_____

2. What footwear are visitors instructed to wear? Why?

_____

3. Is taking pictures during the shipyard tour permissible? Explain.

_____

C Think of situations where items such as in **A** would/wouldn't be allowed. Use the words in the box below to write the <u>rule</u> that people should follow and the <u>reason</u> why they must follow it.

Rule words:
allowed to   permitted to   obligated to   supposed to   required to

Reason words:
because   as   since   due to   so as not to   in order to

Ex.) Rule: You are not <u>allowed to</u> enter the construction site without gloves
     Reason: <u>because</u> sharp or jagged edges might cause serious injuries.

1. Rule: _____

    Reason: _____ .

2. Rule: _____

    Reason: _____ .

3. Rule: _____

    Reason: _____ .

4. Rule: _____

    Reason: _____ .

UNDERSTANDING FLUID AND AIR DYNAMICS

Ken and Lin are studying the differences between airplanes and ships.

Match the words in the box to the following definitions.

| (a) lift | (b) propel | (c) thrust | (d) drag | (e) buoyancy |

1. the force that makes an object float in a fluid   : _____

2. the force from air that pushes against a forward-moving vehicle   : _____

3. the force acting in one direction that pushes an object forward   : _____

4. to drive a vehicle forward   : _____

5. the pressure from air that pushes up on an aircraft's wings   : _____

 Label the forces acting on the airplane and ship in the pictures. Some words are used twice.

| drag | lift | thrust | weight | buoyancy |

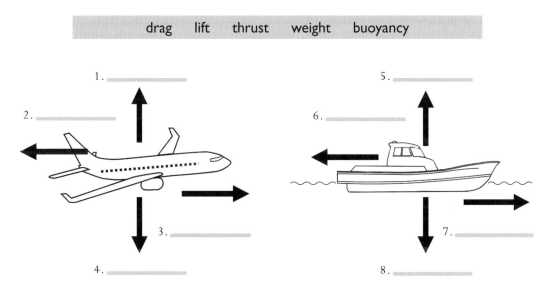

1. _____
2. _____
3. _____
4. _____
5. _____
6. _____
7. _____
8. _____

C Read the dialogue with a partner and answer the questions.

Lin : Hey Ken, did you know that there are boats that can fly through water?

Ken : Do you mean like seaplanes that can take off and land on water?

Lin : No, those are still considered airplanes, not boats. Have you ever heard of hydrofoils?

Ken : No, what's that?

Lin : Well, airplanes' wings are also known as airfoils. And some boats have hydrofoils. You know what? Let me draw what I'm talking about. [draws an airfoil]

Ken : Yeah, sure.

Lin : As you can see here, hydrofoils are attached to struts beneath the main body. Oh, by the way, the main body is also called the hull. You can think of airfoils and hydrofoils operating in similar ways. Now, as you can imagine, the properties of air and water are quite different. However, both air and water are inherently fluids, and so they follow the same fluid laws. With airplanes, lift overcomes weight to make the planes fly. Also, thrust overcomes drag to make them accelerate.

Ken : I see. Well, I know that with airplanes, the teardrop shape of the foils is important. For example … [draws next to Lin's drawing]

Lin : Yes, that's right. The flow of air over the top of the foil is faster than the flow beneath the foil, creating lift.

Ken : But in the case of boats, why do they need foils?

Lin : Well, as you know, ships have speed limitations due to drag. But by installing hydrofoils, we can generate enough lift to raise the hull out of the water. As a result, we can make a ship's hull literally fly, which significantly reduces drag.

Ken : Oh, I see. The hydrofoils reduce drag, and the ship can move faster with greater fuel efficiency. That's amazing!

1. Match the parts of the images below with the vocabulary from the box.

| strut | hull | teardrop | hydrofoil | lift | airflow |

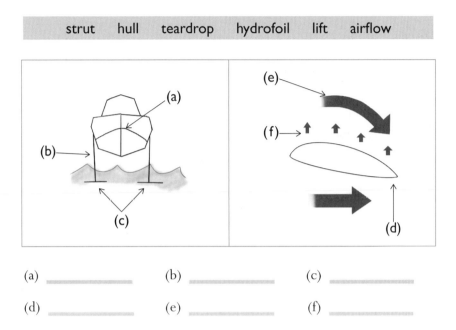

(a) _____   (b) _____   (c) _____

(d) _____   (e) _____   (f) _____

2. Circle True or False for each.
    (a) Hydrofoils and airfoils are both a type of wing to generate lift.
         [True / False]
    (b) The physics of an airfoil and hydrofoil are deduced from different principles.
         [True / False]
    (c) Hydrofoils can make a hull fly in the air.
         [True / False]
    (d) One of the advantages of hydrofoils over conventional boats is their fuel efficiency.
         [True / False]

Read the lecture and match the explanations with the pictures.

Professor:

A bow is the name of the front section of any ship. There are several kinds of bows, but the one in this picture is called a bulbous bow. Can you guess why a bulbous bow is shaped the way it is? Well, compared to a conventional bow such as a clipper bow, a bulbous bow has an added section under the clipper that is beneath the water. What do you think is the purpose of this part? To understand more, let's take apart a bulbous bow and separate it into two parts, the clipper and the bulb, and see how each works. First, what will happen when a clipper bow comes in contact with and passes through water? Well, it will cause a bow wave. Next, let's separate the bulb part from a bulbous bow and move it underneath the water. What will happen? The bulb induces water to flow up and over it, making the water fluctuate. Now, compare the shapes of the waves that the clipper bow and bulb create. As you can see, the crest, or top, of the bow wave corresponds to the trough, or bottom, of the wave created by the bulb. Therefore, the bow wave is offset by the trough. To sum up, by combining a clipper bow and bulb, we can reduce wave resistance against ships.

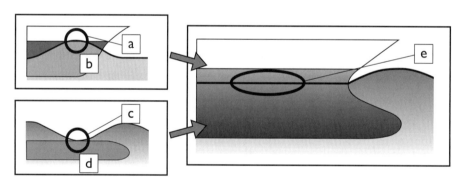

Bulbous Bow

1. profile (shape) of the clipper bow : _____

2. profile (shape) of the bulb : _____

3. wave crest created by the clipper bow : _____

4. wave trough created by the bulb : _____

5. waterline and region of canceled waves : _____

THE CLASS TOURS A SHIPYARD

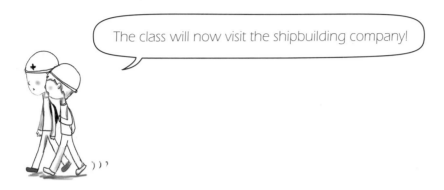

The class will now visit the shipbuilding company!

A Listen to the audio and complete the flowchart for the shipbuilding process.

Bending   Assembling blocks   Painting   Launching   Lofting

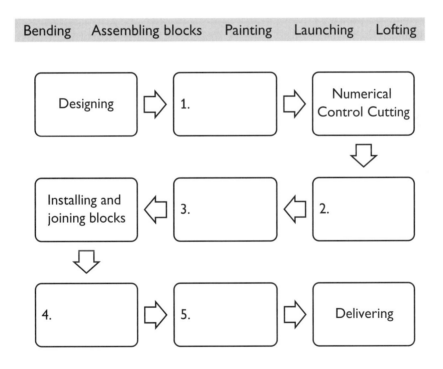

Designing → 1. → Numerical Control Cutting → 2. → 3. → Installing and joining blocks → 4. → 5. → Delivering

B Read the following steps below that are from A and put them in order (1-9).

_1_ : The customer who places an order for a ship is consulted to discuss the basic design. Here, the ship is designed to have high-performance while considering various limitations, and a plan for efficient shipbuilding is made.

___ : The ship finally leaves the shipyard and sets sail into the sea and into the world, seen off by the shipowner and the shipyard staff members. Bon Voyage!

___ : The ship is painted not only for appearances but also for the prevention of corrosion.

___ : The machined steel plates are bent to make the curvy shapes of the ship. They are pressed with a press machine or heated on the surface by a gas burner and bent carefully to match the model. Since automated machines are not proficient enough to make these bends, highly skilled crafts(wo)men are required.

___ : The block construction method is adopted, which divides a ship into blocks according to their size and assembles them separately in a shipyard. The cut and bent parts are welded together and assembled in a three-dimensional block.

___ : The assembled blocks are installed and joined in order on a building berth by a crane and are assembled in the form of the ship. This step requires extra caution, as even a slightly incorrect positioning can lead to serious distortions in the ship.

___ : After completing the painting step, the ship is launched into the water for the first time. The building berth inclines to the direction of the sea, and the ship slides down and floats into the water. The ship will now be equipped with the remaining parts.

___ : Lofting is undergone, a drafting technique to generate curved lines for streamlined things such as airplanes and ships. During this step, the plan to assemble several machined steel plates together is made.

___ : Steel plates for each part of the ship are cut from steel slabs. These used to be cut by hand using a cutting machine, but complicated parts are now automatically cut with a Numerical Control Cutting machine.

C Answer the following questions based on the information in B.

1. What is Numerical Control Cutting?

_____

2. Why is craftsmanship important for shipbuilding? In which step is it especially needed?

_____

3. What is the block construction method?

_____

LEARNING ABOUT CORPORATE SOCIAL RESPONSIBILITY (CSR)

The class is learning about social responsibility for the company.

 Choose the words that are NOT similar to the words in 1-5.

1. retain
   (a) maintain　　(b) possess　　(c) abandon　　(d) keep

2. endeavor
   (a) aspire　　(b) conceal　　(c) strive　　(d) undertake

3. engage
   (a) preoccupy　　(b) involve　　(c) participate　　(d) disgust

4. inclined
   (a) apt　　(b) prone　　(c) resistant　　(d) disposed

5. restore
   (a) decline　　(b) revitalize　　(c) strengthen　　(d) recover

Listen to the company's activities and match them to the mottos.

SETO SHIPBUILDING COMPANY'S MOTTOS

1. _____

2. _____

3. _____

(a) Contributing to local communities
(b) Nurturing future generations
(c) Going green

 Now read some more activities of the company and match them to the mottos in B (a-c).

1. We conduct various research at the shipyard's research center. This includes tidal energy research, which is expected to enable us to produce electricity utilizing clean energy.	_____
2. By holding shipyard tours and launching ceremonies, we occasionally open our shipyards to the public, which is usually restricted to outsiders. In doing so, we provide opportunities to learn more about our industry to attract youth towards shipbuilding careers.	_____
3. We sponsor several local events to vitalize our communities and preserve their culture. We encourage our employees to take part in an annual festival where more than 100 participants perform traditional dancing.	_____

D Discuss the following questions with a partner.

1. Are you familiar with any corporate social responsibility (CSR) activities of companies that you know? If so, explain.
2. If you were to run a company, what kinds of CSR activities would you do? Why?

FOLLOWING A GOVERNMENT-INITIATED PROJECT
i-Shipping

Ken and Lin came back from the tour and are now attending a lecture about i-Shipping.

 Read the following dialogue and handout from the professor and answer the questions.

Professor:

Welcome back, everyone. How was the tour? I hope you enjoyed it and learned a lot. Today I'm going to introduce some changes that have been taking place in shipyards. Has anyone heard of the i-Shipping project? No one? To put it simply, it is a project to find ways to produce ships more efficiently. You've probably heard of smart factories. Well, shipyards are now similarly transforming themselves to become 'smart' by applying information technology. Please take a look at the handout in which I roughly summarized the project.

Summary of the i-Shipping project initiated by the Marine Bureau, Ministry of Land, Infrastructure, Transport and Tourism

Background

Japan had remained the world's largest shipbuilder since 1956, or for about half a century. However, its global market share shrank from 50% to about 20% due to the rise of competition from Korea in the 80s and China in the 90s. Despite the adversity, Japan's strength in productivity and energy-saving technologies has boosted the country higher in the world market in recent years. However, in order to further regain the market share and return to the top, Japan needs to take advantage of its strength in productivity while overcoming its weakness in cost competitiveness.

Objective

The i-Shipping project aims to revitalize the Japanese marine industries (shipbuilding and marine transportation) to be cost-competitive in the world markets, produce high-quality products, and deliver high-quality service. It supports the maritime industries with research and development and puts into practice revolutionary technologies and systems to increase productivity utilizing information technologies such as the Internet of things (IoT), big data, and AI.

Reference:
Ministry of Land, Infrastructure, Transport and Tourism (http://www.mlit.go.jp/common/001133769.pdf)

1. What is the aim of the i-Shipping project?

_____

_____

2. What is the context behind the bureau's decision to initiate the project?

_____

_____

3. What is the key to increasing the productivity of shipbuilding?

_____

 Read the handout and fill in the blanks with the most appropriate words in the box. Use each word only once.

Professor:

Let's now move on to concrete activities for the project, which are comprised of three pillars: design, production, and operation. Please take a look at the handout.

A part of the handout

> **i-Shipping: Design**
>
> In order to design new high-performance ships and quickly develop them, the project promotes the following research:
> - developing a method to 1. (deny / simulate) water flow around designed ships
> - establishing international standards for 2. (valid / false) assessment of ship performance based on simulations to prevent fraud
>
> The project also promotes joint-usage experimental facilities such as towing tanks to accelerate research.
>
>

i-Shipping: Production

In order to improve 3. (transparency / uncertainty), the project promotes research and development to streamline the flow of people and things involved in the manufacturing processes based on IoT technology. Some examples include:
- efficient inventory management by using RFID tags
- efficient and secure management of the field workforce using sensors and monitors

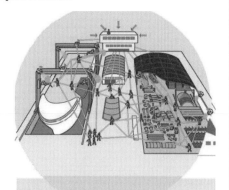

The project encourages the 4. (collapse / investment) into the automation of manufacturing processes such as automatic welding systems.

i-Shipping: Operation

To enhance service quality, the project promotes the following research and development based on IoT technology and big data analytics by:
- developing a preventive maintenance system using sensors to detect or 5. (maintain / anticipate) the wear and malfunction of ship components
- developing a ship routing 6. (decline / optimization) system based on the analysis of weather and hydrographic conditions

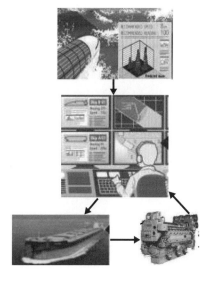

Reference: ibid.

Ken learned a lot throughout the shipyard tour. He is now more interested in how products are produced at companies.

Manufacturing, Assembly, and Components

Ken will visit two companies!

INTRODUCTION
PARTICIPATING IN A SPECIAL PROGRAM

 Listen to Ken's update and discuss the questions with a partner.

1. What will Ken do in this unit?

2. Have you ever taken part in a company tour or internship before? If so, explain it.

3. What type of company would you like to tour if you have the opportunity? Why?

Ken is meeting Lin and her friend on campus.

B Listen to the conversation and fill in the blanks with what you hear.

Ken : Hey, Lin! What's going on?

Lin : Hi, Ken! Nothing much. How have you been since I last saw you? I haven't seen you in a while.

Ken : I've been very busy **1.**_____ _____ attending classes and doing lab work. Oh, and research on top of that.

Lin : I know exactly what you mean! Actually, I'm pretty busy as well. By the way, have you met Luke?

Luke: **2.**_____ _____ _____ Ken. Lin told me that she made a new Japanese friend. It's nice to meet you.

Ken : Hi, Luke! It's nice to meet you, too. So, what are you guys up to today?

Lin : We just **3.**_____ _____ about a special program that offers one-day internships at manufacturing companies. Have you heard about it?

Ken : No, I haven't. But I thought your major was Ocean Engineering.

Lin : Yeah, it is. But it's open to any technical majors. We just have to attend a lecture on manufacturing first before we can **4.**_____ _____ in it.

Luke: It seems like a great opportunity to learn about the industry and get to experience real companies. Plus, it would look good on our resumes!

Lin : **5.**_____ _____ _____? Ken, why don't you join as well? It'll be fun!

Ken : Oh, I don't know. I'm not sure if I'm **6.**_____ _____ _____. I mean, I'm already so busy and all.

Luke: Well, it's up to you. But it seems like it would be very beneficial if you can make it.

Ken : Yeah, it seems interesting. I'll have to think about it.

C Complete the sentences by unscrambling the expressions.

1. _____ _____ _____ _____. I've heard a lot about you.
   (a) Ken   (b) you   (c) be   (d) must

2. _____ _____ _____? _____ think that is a great idea!
   (a) you   (b) I   (c) what   (d) know

3. You are full _____ _____, _____ _____.
    (a) of   (b) usual   (c) energy   (d) as

4. I've been so tired lately. I don't _____ _____ _____ _____.
    (a) up   (b) anything   (c) for   (d) feel

ATTENDING A LECTURE   BASICS OF MACHINING

Ken decided to join a special program and is attending a lecture on machining.

 Match the words in the box to each description.

(a) machine   (b) chip   (c) coolant   (d) aid   (e) discharge

1. This is when you help someone do something.   : ____

2. To make or shape something, you _____ it.   : ____

3. This is a small piece of wood, stone, metal, etc. that has been broken off. : ____

4. This is a liquid or gas used to lower the temperature of an engine.   : ____

5. This is when electrical equipment sends out electricity.   : ____

(f) torch   (g) arc   (h) erosion   (i) distortion   (j) net

6. This is the process by which something is gradually reduced or destroyed.   : _____

7. This is when an object's shape has changed from its true form.   : _____

8. This is a long stick with burning material at one end.   : _____

9. A _____ result is the final result after all details have been considered.   : _____

10. This is a flash of light formed by the flow of electricity between two points.   : _____

 B Listen to the explanation and fill in the blanks with some of the words you learned.

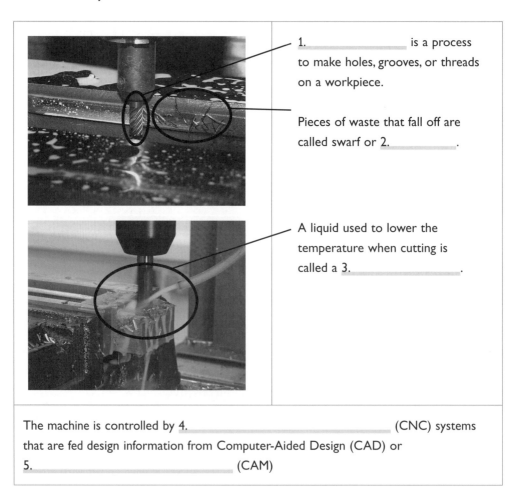

1. _____ is a process to make holes, grooves, or threads on a workpiece.

Pieces of waste that fall off are called swarf or 2. _____ .

A liquid used to lower the temperature when cutting is called a 3. _____ .

The machine is controlled by 4. _____ (CNC) systems that are fed design information from Computer-Aided Design (CAD) or 5. _____ (CAM)

Read the professor's explanation and answer the questions.

Professor:

We have finished going through the basics of machining. Let's now move on to specific ways of machining. What do you think are the key factors in determining the most appropriate cutting method? Well, we first need to think about the properties of the material you want to machine. Specifically, we should consider the material's thermal, electrical, and mechanical properties. This includes the thickness, shape, and complexity of the workpiece. For example, when cutting materials using high pressure, we have to consider if the material can bear the mechanical stress. Additionally, if we cut a material with heat to melt it, we will need to address heat-affected zones, or heat distortion. We must also consider the required edge quality. For instance, can we make an initial rough cut, or does it need to be precise on the first cut? Therefore, when choosing a cutting method, we have to consider if it requires a secondary operation or not. If the cut edge is rough, we will need to make additional cuts to smoothen it out. Given these requirements, it is important to think about how to produce net-shaped components efficiently.

1. What are the main factors when deciding the appropriate cutting method?

   _____

2. What do we need to consider when cutting a material using high pressure?

   _____

3. If you are cutting a material using heat to melt it, what needs to be addressed?

   _____

4. What is a secondary operation?

   _____

Below are several machining methods. Read the descriptions and write the correct machining methods from the box.

Flame cutting   Plasma cutting   Electric discharge machining (EDM)
Ultra high-pressure water jet cutting   Guillotining

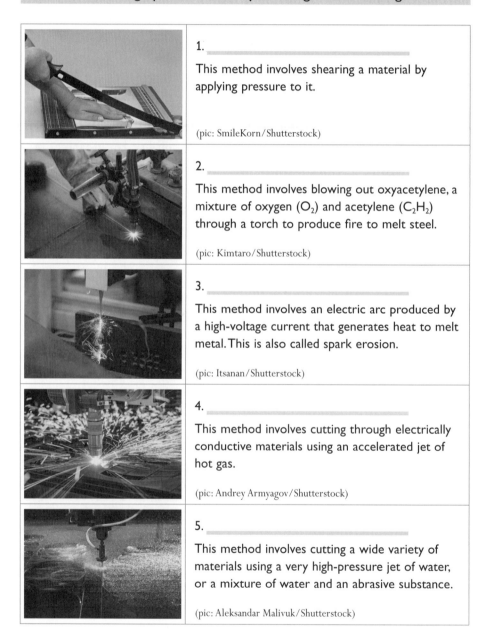

1. _____

This method involves shearing a material by applying pressure to it.

(pic: SmileKorn/Shutterstock)

2. _____

This method involves blowing out oxyacetylene, a mixture of oxygen (O_2) and acetylene (C_2H_2) through a torch to produce fire to melt steel.

(pic: Kimtaro/Shutterstock)

3. _____

This method involves an electric arc produced by a high-voltage current that generates heat to melt metal. This is also called spark erosion.

(pic: Itsanan/Shutterstock)

4. _____

This method involves cutting through electrically conductive materials using an accelerated jet of hot gas.

(pic: Andrey Armyagov/Shutterstock)

5. _____

This method involves cutting a wide variety of materials using a very high-pressure jet of water, or a mixture of water and an abrasive substance.

(pic: Aleksandar Malivuk/Shutterstock)

LEARNING JOINING TECHNIQUES AT A COMPANY

Ken, Lin, and Luke are now studying the processes of joining before visiting a company.

A Listen to the conversation and complete the table. First, fill in the categories for 1-2. Then choose the appropriate joining methods for 3-6.

	adhesives screws rivets welding		

		Mechanical	1. _____
Temporary		Ex.) nuts and bolts 3. _____	
2. _____		4. _____	5. _____ 6. _____

B Ken and Luke are talking about the company that they will visit. Listen to their conversation and answer the questions.

1. What is Hardlock?
   (a) a company named after a café
   (b) a company that manufactures traditional wedges
   (c) a company that produces nuts and bolts

2. What is Hardlock well-known for?
   (a) manufacturing bullet trains
   (b) using traditional wooden wedges
   (c) manufacturing a product that won't loosen

3. What is the purpose of inserting a wedge?
    (a) to tightly connect two pieces
    (b) to separate two pieces
    (c) to cut a piece in half

4. Match the letters in the image (a-d) with the correct
    words below.

    mortise: _____   tenon: _____

    gap: _____   wedge: _____

C The three are now visiting Hardlock Industries. Read and complete
the summary note. Review *B* if necessary.

The typical reason fasteners become loose is because of the play between the nut
and bolt. Play is the extra space between two objects, and when there is too much play,
vibrations and shock can make the nut and bolt loosen. By completely eliminating the
play, it is possible to achieve an ideal looseness-prevention mechanism. Through much
research, Hardlock has developed a fastener in which the traditional Japanese wedge
principle is applied to nuts. This revolutionary product is the HLN Hardlock Nut.

The HLN Hardlock Nut is actually composed of two nuts, one that is convex-
shaped and one that is concave-shaped. The convex and concave nuts are brought
together to mechanically generate a powerful locking effect transverse to the bolt shaft
utilizing the wedge principle. The HLN Hardlock Nut wedge creates a powerful
looseness-prevention effect, completely fusing the nut and bolt together to shield the
fastener from all vibrations and shock.

(Source: https://www.hardlock.co.jp/en/technical-info/principle/)

Conventional nut and bolt

1.＿＿＿ and 2.＿＿＿ cause the nut and bolt to loosen because there is extra space between them, known as 3.＿＿＿.	

Hardlock's nut and bolt

The key to preventing loosening is in dividing the nut into two parts and applying the wedge principle. The concave-shaped nut serves as a mortise and the bolt as a tenon. The other part of the nut, which is convex-shaped, functions as a 4.＿＿＿ and is inserted into the gap between the mortise and tenon. This eliminates the space between the nut and bolt and creates a powerful locking effect 5.＿＿＿ to the shaft.	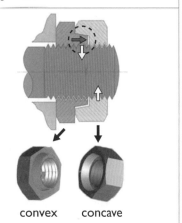 convex concave

UNDERSTANDING THE BACKGROUND
SMART MANUFACTURING

Ken and Lin are doing some background research on manufacturing to prepare for the next visit.

SMART MANUFACTURING

Read the following and fill in the blanks with the most appropriate words from the box. Use each word only once.

enable	encompasses	integrated	perceived	put

Professor:

So far, we have discussed several processes involved in manufacturing, such as machining and joining. Now, let's move to the bigger picture of manufacturing. Today's topic is the newly emerging conceptualization of manufacturing, namely smart manufacturing. To **1.** _____ it simply, smart manufacturing is interconnected manufacturing systems in which information technologies are **2.** _____ into operation technologies with the purpose of optimizing manufacturing processes. In smart manufacturing, any discrete processes concerning manufacturing can be networked together by computers, which transforms our conventional view of manufacturing. Traditionally, manufacturing was **3.** _____ to be a system accomplished on a factory floor. In contrast, smart manufacturing involves a product life-cycle view that **4.** _____ not just the manufacturing processes in a factory but a whole supply chain. It ranges from product design and raw material procurement to product distribution and even recycling. The interconnected systems **5.** _____ manufacturers to flexibly respond to changes in demand with minimal cost and no damage to the environment.

 Read the articles and choose True or False for each statement.

Professor:

Smart manufacturing covers many different technologies. Even though it is broadly defined, most of the definitions embrace the following as the key technologies.

Big data analytics

One of the key technologies that differentiates smart manufacturing from conventional manufacturing is the way of collecting and processing data. In conventional manufacturing, information about individual manufacturing machines was **accumulated** in local databases and used only to improve the performance of each of them. In smart manufacturing, all of the data in terms of complicated manufacturing processes and supply chains are **compiled** and analyzed in order to **refine** them. The utilization of big data and its analysis allows

---

a manufacturing enterprise to shift from reactionary practices to predictive ones; it enables improvements to the efficiency of processes and also the performance of the products. Big data analytics refers to a method for compiling and understanding large data-sets. It concerns three parameters, or so-called three V's: volume, velocity, and variety. Volume represents the amount of data, velocity describes the frequency of data generation and acquisition, and variety pertains to the capability of handling several types of incoming data.

Smart machines

Another key technology for smart manufacturing is advanced robots known as smart machines. A prominent characteristic of smart machines is that they can operate autonomously, meaning that they are able to complete work by themselves. In addition, artificial intelligence enables robots to learn from past experiences and thereby do more than they were initially programmed to do. It allows the robots to flexibly reconfigure or repurpose themselves and make decisions to solve problems. As a consequence, manufacturers can respond quicker than ever to changes in design or demand, giving them a competitive advantage over ones working with traditional manufacturing processes. Despite such advantages, there are also some disadvantages. One concern is the safety and well-being of human workers **interacting** with robotic systems. To protect individuals, manufacturers have **isolated** robots from humans. Yet current research is expanding the possibility for robots to work collaboratively with humans.

1. Big data analytics enables companies to not only respond to orders placed but also to anticipate demand.

   [True / False]

2. Big data processing involves gathering and interpreting large data-sets.

   [True / False]

3. Smart machines are designed to work by themselves without the help of humans.

   [True / False]

4. The purpose of installing AI in advanced robots is to prevent them from acting too autonomously.

   [True / False]

5. People always work better alongside robots than when segregated from them.

   [True / False]

Review the boldfaced vocabulary in and choose the words that are NOT similar to them.

1. accumulate
   (a) diminish   (b) increase   (c) expand   (d) collect

2. compile
   (a) gather   (b) collect   (c) assemble   (d) distribute

3. refine
   (a) improve   (b) cultivate   (c) aggravate   (d) polish

4. interact
   (a) communicate   (b) divide   (c) cooperate   (d) merge

5. isolate
   (a) segregate   (b) attach   (c) separate   (d) confine

Discuss the following questions with a partner.

1. What type of data needs to be collected and processed to realize smart manufacturing?
2. What can robots do better than humans? What can humans do better than robots?
3. In what ways can robots and humans cooperate and work together?

VISITING A STEEL COMPANY

Ken, Lin, and Luke are now visiting the second company, Kansai Steel Co., which has great potential for contributing to the realization of smart manufacturing in shipyards.

 Listen to the audio. Fill in the blanks using the items in the box.

(a) titanium   (b) wire rods and bars   (c) standard compressors
(d) ultra high-pressure equipment   (e) robots and electric power sources

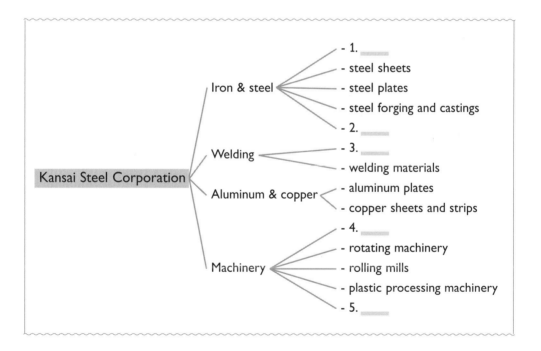

Kansai Steel Corporation

Iron & steel
- 1. _____
- steel sheets
- steel plates
- steel forging and castings
- 2. _____

Welding
- 3. _____
- welding materials

Aluminum & copper
- aluminum plates
- copper sheets and strips

Machinery
- 4. _____
- rotating machinery
- rolling mills
- plastic processing machinery
- 5. _____

Read the next part of the handout and answer the questions.

Tour guide:
This section explains the three parts of our shipyard automatic welding system.

AUTOMATIC WELDING SYSTEM

SMART WELDING

Despite the efforts of shipbuilding companies to automate the shipbuilding process, it has been difficult to incorporate an automatic welding system into the block assembling process. This is due to the fact that each component has a unique shape. However, we have developed software that can analyze 3D-CAD ship drawings, generate welding lines, and provide instructions to the welding robots.

WELDING ROBOT

There is not enough workspace to install conventional welding machines in a shipyard. We solved this issue by inventing a welding robot that is 78% smaller than conventional ones. The new robot can work in small spaces while still remaining reliable and durable.

MANUFACTURING MANAGEMENT

We created a manufacturing system based on IoT technologies to increase the efficiency of welding. By collecting data from the welding conditions of the robots and issues occurring within the process of manufacturing, we can improve the quality of our products.

---

1. What is the difficulty in introducing an automatic welding system to the block assembling step of shipbuilding?

2. Why is it necessary to have miniaturized welding robots?

3. How is IoT technology used?

WORKING ON A PROJECT AT THE COMPANY

touch base ...
give me a hand ...
hold off ...
count on ...

Ken is practicing some useful work-related expressions in order to do well on the project.

 First, choose the appropriate words to complete the example sentences. Then match the sentences with their meanings.

Example sentence	Meaning
Ex.) He is taking ((on) / into / under) the project.	when someone receives more responsibility or work
1. Why don't you think it (under / on / over) and let me know tomorrow?	when something has good results and progress is moving forward
2. Did you follow (through / in / under) on the task I gave you?	when someone completes their responsibility or task
3. Everything is fine and the project is (coming / leaving / going) well.	to consider something before accepting it

The three are working on a project together as part of the one-day internship.

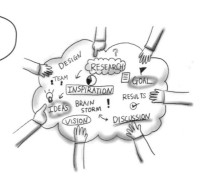

B Ken overheard some employees at the company discussing work. Listen and write what you hear. Then compare your answers with a partner.

1. _____

_____

2. _____

_____

3. _____

_____

4. _____

_____

C What do you think the following expressions mean? Select the letters with the closest meaning of the boldfaced words.

1. Hey Chris, I wanted to **touch base** with you regarding the project that you are working on.
   (a) I want to talk to you about the project and get an update.
   (b) I want you to finish and submit the project soon.
   (c) I want you to help me with the project.

2. Could you **give me a hand** with this project?
   (a) Can you give me the details of the project?
   (b) Can you help me with the project?
   (c) Can you turn the project in?

3. For now, please **hold off on** doing it.
   (a) Please try your hardest.
   (b) Please don't do it now.
   (c) Please do it carefully.

4. Don't worry about it. You can **count on** me!

   (a) If I can do it, then you can too.

   (b) Please ask someone else if you have any questions.

   (c) You can rely on me.

 Listen to a manager and choose an appropriate response.

   1. (a) (b) (c)   2. (a) (b) (c)   3. (a) (b) (c)   4. (a) (b) (c)

Ken successfully completed the program! During the closing ceremony, he talked with employees from both companies and learned that the corporate world is now drastically globalizing and that presenting one's idea in English is more important than ever.

Materials Science

Ken will take part in an international conference where he'll meet up with a friend!

INTRODUCTION   RECEIVING AN EMAIL FROM JOHN

 Listen to Ken's update and number the following in the order that the information is given.

$$1^{st} \text{ (a) } \Rightarrow 2^{nd} \underline{\qquad} \Rightarrow 3^{rd} \underline{\qquad} \Rightarrow 4^{th} \underline{\qquad} \Rightarrow 5^{th} \underline{\qquad}$$

To: Ken

From: John

Dear Ken,

How have you been?

Three months have passed since I came back to Singapore. **1.**_____ I already miss Osaka Tech University and Japan. I am really hoping to come back and visit someday! By the way, I attended a conference in Singapore and presented my research results from your lab. I was very nervous before the presentation because it was my first time presenting research. But I somehow managed to **2.**_____.

Oh, and guess what? At that conference, I **3.**_____ some professors from your university! I talked to them, and it turns out that one of them knows your supervisor. I think it would be great if we could meet up like that someday! If you get a chance to come to Singapore, please contact me! I would definitely show you around. I will never forget your kindness!

4._____. **5.**_____ your lab mates and the professor.

Sincerely,

John

1. (a) Practice makes perfect!   (b) Better late than never!   (c) Time flies!
2. (a) get to   (b) get by   (c) drop by
3. (a) walked in on   (b) ran on   (c) ran into
4. (a) Please do me a favor   (b) Please ask a favor of me   (c) You bother me
5. (a) help me forget   (b) send my regards to   (c) catch up with

BACKGROUND SEARCHING
FINDING A CONFERENCE TO ATTEND

Ken is searching online for a conference.

 Listen to the conversation between Ken and Lin while looking at the webpage below. Then answer the questions.

https://www.conferencefinder.com

Upcoming conferences

Country		Theme
Asia	**North/South America**	Business Management
China	United States	Biochemistry
India	Canada	Chemical Engineering
Indonesia	Mexico	Chemistry
Malaysia	Brazil	Electrical & Electronics
The Philippines	**Europe**	Engineering
Singapore	France	Environmental Sciences
South Korea	Italy	Materials Science
Thailand	Germany	Microbiology
Pacific	The Netherlands	Nanotechnology
Australia	Spain	Neuroscience
New Zealand	UK	Pharmaceutical Sciences
		Physics

1. Which is Lin's recommendation concerning the country of the conference?
   (a) Germany   (b) United States   (c) Indonesia   (d) Malaysia

2. Which conference theme is Ken thinking about choosing?
   (a) Materials Science   (b) Chemical Engineering
   (c) Electrical & Electronics Engineering   (d) Business Management

3. What will Ken do before deciding on the conference?
   (a) email John   (b) finish his research
   (c) study English   (d) talk to Lin's professor

 B Discuss the following questions with a partner.

1. Have you ever attended a conference before? If so, what type of conference was it?
2. Would you like to give a presentation in the future? Why/why not?
3. What conference themes are you interested in? Why?

 C Ken is now looking at the conference's website. Skim the information and circle True or False regarding the statements.

https://www.acms.com

The 10ᵗʰ Asian Conference on Materials Science
March 20ᵗʰ-22ⁿᵈ in Singapore
Call for papers

We warmly welcome you to join us for the 10ᵗʰ Asian Conference on Materials Science at Nanyang University in Singapore. The conference aims to promote breakthrough developments in the fields of chemistry, physics, materials science, and engineering to address technology needs. Scientists, entrepreneurs, faculty, and students with different backgrounds and expertise from all over the world will convene to present their latest research, attend various workshops, and engage in stimulating dialogues during the reception.
[…]

Abstract submission deadline	**Registration information**
First round (for all types of presentations): ~~July 20th~~ *Now closed*	Registration is now open. Please enroll soon to get our early bird price. Students are also eligible to receive a reduced registration price.
Late submissions (for all types of presentations): ~~October 15th~~ *Now closed*	- Early bird registration: before January 31st - Regular registration: before February 28th
Final deadline (only for regular presentations and poster presentations): ~~January 10th~~ *Extended to Jan. 15th*	*Note that online registration in advance is required to take part in the conference. On-site registration is not available.

1. People with backgrounds in both academia and business will join the conference.

   [True / False]

2. If Ken wants to participate in a poster presentation, he must submit his abstract on or before October 15th.

   [True / False]

3. Those who register early will receive a discount on the registration fee.

   [True / False]

4. Registering in advance is not mandatory but optional for students.

   [True / False]

SIGNING UP FOR A CONFERENCE

Ken talked to Lin's professor about the conference and was encouraged to join it!

Read Ken's abstract and answer the questions with a partner.

Limit Load and Failure Mechanisms of Material X

Ken Nakamura

Material X is widely used in the industry as an insulating material. However, its mechanical properties are not well investigated yet. This research proposes a new method for increasing the limit of Material X's load capacity, which is naturally fragile and sensitive to mechanical and thermal loading conditions. In this research, three different methods of load applications on Material X and their influence on failure mechanisms are investigated in detail. The results of the numerical analysis, based on tensile strength tests, indicate the significance of the specimen size and shape effects on the strength of the material.

[…]

In conclusion, a careful adjustment of the size and shape of properties is the main factor in extending the load limits of Material X in engineering applications.

References

[…]

---

1. What is the background of Ken's research?

2. What is the purpose of Ken's research?

3. What properties does Material X have?

B After finishing his abstract, Ken is now submitting it online. Listen to the audio and circle or write what he put for each part.

---

1. Name: (NAKAMURA, Ken)   (Ken Nakamura)

2. Affiliation: (Graduate School of Engineering, Osaka Tech University)

                             (Osaka Tech University)

                             (Osaka Tech University, Graduate School of Engineering)

3. Telephone: (06-6879-555)   (0806-6879-555)   (86-6879-555)

4. Email: knakamura@_____

5. Type of presentation: _____

 C Ken received several emails from the conference coordinator after submitting his proposal. Organize them in the order they were received.

$$1^{st} \ (a) \Rightarrow 2^{nd} \underline{\quad} \Rightarrow 3^{rd} \underline{\quad} \Rightarrow 4^{th} \underline{\quad} \Rightarrow 5^{th} \underline{\quad}$$

(a)

To: Ken Nakamura

From: Stephen Levinson

Dear Mr. Nakamura,

Thank you for registering for an account on our website. Please note that this email does not represent confirmation of any proposal submissions. If you would like to submit a proposal, please follow the indicated instructions and email the appropriate materials by the deadline.

[...]

(b)

To: Ken Nakamura

From: Stephen Levinson

Dear Mr. Nakamura,

The day of the conference is fast approaching and just two weeks are remaining. To make sure that everything goes smoothly, we would like to remind you of the things that you are expected to bring with you on the day.
[...]

(c)

To: Ken Nakamura

From: Stephen Levinson

Dear Mr. Nakamura,

After a thorough review by the conference organizers, we are pleased to inform you that your submission for a poster presentation has been accepted. Please consider this email our formal congratulations! Please take a moment to look over the comments from the reviewers by logging in to our website. It is essential that you take these comments into account when preparing the final version.
[...]

(d)

To: Ken Nakamura

From: Stephen Levinson

Dear Mr. Nakamura,

Your poster presentation proposal, Limit Load and Failure Mechanisms of Material X, is still under peer-review. We apologize for the wait. The result will be sent out shortly.
[...]

(e)

To: Ken Nakamura

From: Stephen Levinson

Dear Mr. Nakamura,

Thank you for your proposal submission to the 10th Asian Conference on Materials Science. This email is confirmation that we have received your poster presentation proposal entitled Limit Load and Failure Mechanisms of Material X. We will review the proposal and inform you of our decision at a later date. If you need to make changes, you can do so on the conference website before October 15th. Please visit our website for details.

[...]

𝒟 Put the words in the right order to complete the sentences.

1. _____ _____ _____, _____ mainly discuss the thermal properties of the material.

   (a) follows   (b) what   (c) in   (d) we

2. Please _____ _____ _____ _____ changes to your address as soon as possible.

   (a) any   (b) of   (c) us   (d) inform

3. Due to several requests, we've decided to _____ _____ _____ _____ the conference schedule.

   (a) to   (b) a   (c) make   (d) change

4. Did you _____ _____ _____ _____ necessary procedures to successfully conduct the experiment?

   (a) into   (b) take   (c) account   (d) the

5. Under these heating conditions, the material _____ _____ _____ _____ 150 degrees Celsius.

   (a) is   (b) expected   (c) reach   (d) to

PREPARING FOR A POSTER PRESENTATION

> Ken is now learning basic expressions for materials to prepare for his presentation.

A Complete the sentences by choosing the correct substances from Box A and any of the expressions from Box B.

Box A	compound	mixture	element	alloy
Box B	composed of	comprised of	made up of	consists of

Ex.) Water is **a compound**; it **is composed of** hydrogen and oxygen.

1. Sodium is _____ .

2. Salt is _____ ; _____ .

3. Brine is _____ ; _____ .

4. Bronze is _____ ; _____ .

B The mechanical properties of materials are expressed with specific terms. Listen to the explanation and circle the correct words.

I.

If materials are exposed to forces, their shape may change. This is called deformation.

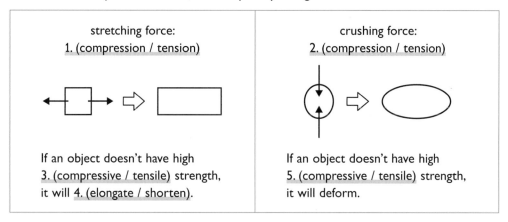

stretching force: 1. (compression / tension)	crushing force: 2. (compression / tension)
If an object doesn't have high 3. (compressive / tensile) strength, it will 4. (elongate / shorten).	If an object doesn't have high 5. (compressive / tensile) strength, it will deform.

The 6. (compressive / tensile) strength of a material is usually lower than the 7. (compressive / tensile) strength.

II.

There are two types of deformation.
If a material is stretched and then it returns to its original shape, it is 8. (elastic / plastic).

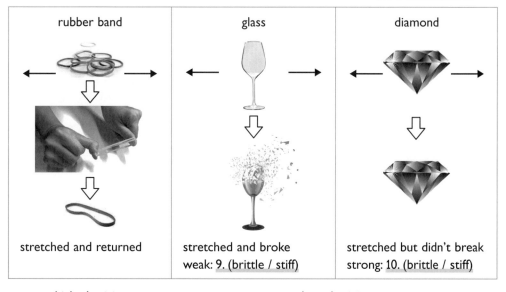

rubber band	glass	diamond
stretched and returned	stretched and broke weak: 9. (brittle / stiff)	stretched but didn't break strong: 10. (brittle / stiff)

high elasticity ◄─────────► low elasticity

If a material is deformed and does not return to its original shape, it is 11. (elastic / plastic)

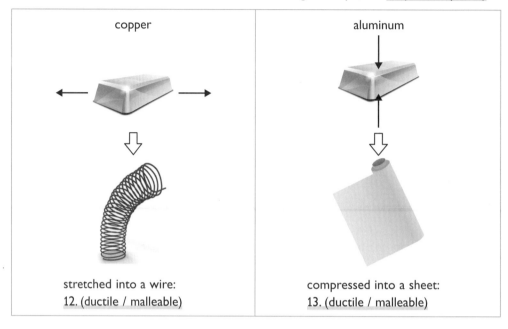

copper

stretched into a wire:
12. (ductile / malleable)

aluminum

compressed into a sheet:
13. (ductile / malleable)

III.

Whether a material is hard or not is important since it affects the 14. (durability / reliability) of an object. In general, 15. (soft / hard) materials last longer than 16. (soft / hard) materials.

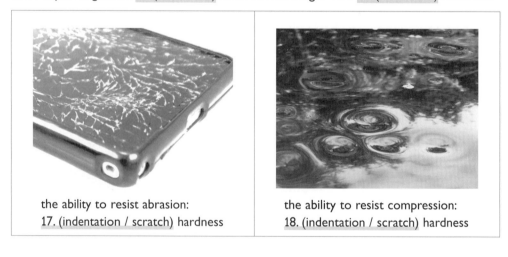

the ability to resist abrasion:
17. (indentation / scratch) hardness

the ability to resist compression:
18. (indentation / scratch) hardness

C Learn the basic properties of materials. Listen to the explanation and match the five properties with the explanations and examples.

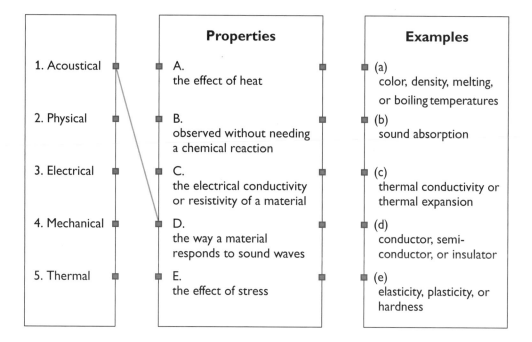

1. Acoustical	**Properties**	**Examples**
2. Physical	A. the effect of heat	(a) color, density, melting, or boiling temperatures
3. Electrical	B. observed without needing a chemical reaction	(b) sound absorption
4. Mechanical	C. the electrical conductivity or resistivity of a material	(c) thermal conductivity or thermal expansion
5. Thermal	D. the way a material responds to sound waves	(d) conductor, semi-conductor, or insulator
	E. the effect of stress	(e) elasticity, plasticity, or hardness

 D Think of a product you use every day. Work with a partner to take turns describing it and guessing what it is. Explain the following.

1. What materials is the product made up of, and what is its purpose?
2. What properties does the product have based on **C**?

GIVING A PRESENTATION

Long time no see!

Ken will fly to Singapore to join the conference. There, he'll meet up with John.

 A Listen to the audio and match what you hear with the equations.

(a) 1.5×10^5	(b) $x \leq y$	(c) $\sqrt{3}$	(d) $x \neq y$
(e) $\frac{3}{4}$	(f) $x \approx y$	(g) $x \propto y$	(h) -25.68%

1. _____   2. _____   3. _____   4. _____

5. _____   6. _____   7. _____   8. _____

 B Read the dialogue about Ken's poster presentation with a partner and fill in the blanks with letters (a-f).

John : Hi, Ken! Long time no see!

Ken : Hi, John! I am really happy to see you again! Thank you for coming to see my presentation.

John : Sure. I also came with several lab mates and Professor Chen. Professor Chen, this is Ken Nakamura. He took good care of me when I studied in Japan. Ken, this is Professor Chen. He is one of my supervisors in my lab.

Ken : Nice to meet you all. I am Ken Nakamura from Osaka Tech University.

John : The research that you're presenting seems to be interesting. Would you like to go ahead and give us your poster presentation?

Ken : OK. Allow me to began. In this research, we examine the failure mechanism of Material X. As you may know, Material X is widely used in many industries.

[…]

Now, look at the figure here that shows the behavior of Material X during the tensile strength tests we conducted.

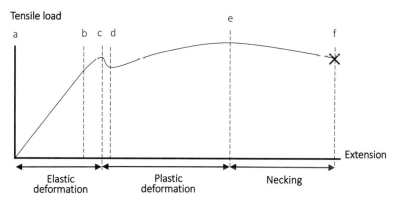

Figure 1: The results of the tensile strength test on Material X

Ex.) From point a to point b, the extension of the Material X sample is proportional to the increase in tension.

1. At point _____, the sample reaches the lower yield point. After this, it continues to incrcase in length with minimal increases in tension.

2. At point _____, the elastic limit is reached, which is known as the upper yield point. Beyond this point, the sample can no longer return to its original length and will begin to plastically deform.

3. At point _____, the sample finally reaches the fracture point and it breaks into two.

4. At point _____, the sample reaches the limit of proportionality. Beyond this point, its extension will start to increase at a slightly greater rate than tension.

5. Point _____ indicates the ultimate tensile strength (UTS) of the sample. This is the maximum tensile load that the sample can bear without breaking. The sample will begin necking if it goes beyond this point.

WATCHING A PLENARY

 Match the words below with their definitions.

1. compensate: _____
2. inhibit : _____
3. discrete: _____
4. reinforce: _____
5. dominate: _____
6. versatile: _____
7. constituent: _____
8. distinctive: _____

(a) having many different uses
(b) preventing something from developing
(c) a part of a whole
(d) having a special quality
(e) to have power or influence over something
(f) balancing the effect of something bad
(g) something that is clearly separated
(h) making something stronger

 Ken and John are listening to a plenary speaker. Read her speech and answer the questions.

Professor Gu:

When you hear the term, composite materials, some of you probably think of the carbon fiber used in aerospace and Formula 1 vehicles. Carbon fiber is surely one of the promising composite materials. But what is the earliest example of man-made composite materials? The answer is bricks used in ancient times to build houses.

Now, how can bricks be considered a composite material? Well, bricks that are only from mud are still very sturdy, meaning they are resistant to crushing force. However, they do have a weakness. Despite their compressive strength, they can be easily broken and pulled apart if bent, as they have poor tensile strength. To inhibit such crumbling, ancient people embedded straw into the mud bricks. In contrast to mud, straw is resistant to stretching force and therefore has excellent tensile strength. But it is very weak when crumpled or crushed. By combining the two, ancient people compensated for the weaknesses of discrete materials. We can now see that bricks made of mud and straw are a composite material; they have a matrix with an internal reinforcing material. The straw acts as the reinforcement, the structural network reinforcing the inside. The mud acts as the matrix, the material surrounding the reinforcement.

Let's move on to fiberglass, or glass-reinforced plastic (GRP) to be precise. Just like bricks, fiberglass is also comprised of two constituents: a plastic matrix reinforced with glass fibers. Glass fibers dominate the reinforced polymer industry and are among the most versatile fibers available. They are used in ship hulls, airfoils, auto bodies, traffic lights, water pipes, and many other applications. Depending on the raw materials used and their proportion, the resulting product will have distinctive characteristics. The properties of several types of glass fibers can be seen in the table.

Glass Fiber Type	Density (g/cm³)	Tensile Strength (MPa)	Elongation (%)	Thermal Expansion Coefficient (10⁻⁷/°C)	Characteristics
A-glass	2.44	3300	4.8	72	high durability
C-glass	2.56	3300	4.8	62	high chemical resistance
E-glass	2.54	3440	4.9	52	high tensile strength & electrical resistivity
S-glass	2.53	4900	5.6	15	high tensile strength

1. Why did ancient people mix straw into mud bricks?

2. Why can we say that bricks are a composite material?

3. What is fiberglass used for?

4. Among the four types of glass fibers, which is the most suitable to use in corrosive acid environments? Why?

5. Among the four types of glass fibers, which extends the most when undergoing tension? Why?

6. Among the four types of glass fibers, which changes the most when heated? Why?

After successfully presenting at the conference, Ken went to dinner with John and his friends to catch up and talk about their future careers.

Applying for an Internship

unit 10

Biotechnology and Applied Chemistry

Ken is thinking about his career after graduation.

INTRODUCTION
THINKING ABOUT FUTURE CAREERS

 Listen to Ken's update and select the correct answer.

1. What was Ken's original plan after graduation?

   (a) He wanted to work for a company in Japan.

   (b) He wanted to continue his research through a doctoral program.

   (c) He wanted to study in the United States.

   (d) He wanted to be a science teacher.

2. Which factor does NOT change Ken's mind regarding his future career?

   (a) welcoming John

   (b) visiting the United States

   (c) joining the international conference

   (d) advice Ken received from his professor

3. Where does Ken want to intern at?

   (a) Southeast Asia

   (b) Europe

   (c) The United States

   (d) Japan

4. Which is NOT a reason why Ken is interested in Polymer Excellence?

   (a) Ken wants to be able to take advantage of his research interest.

   (b) Polymer Excellence is located in the region where Ken would like to go.

   (c) Ken wants to gain experience in a company that produces materials for vehicles or computers.

   (d) Polymer Excellence is internationally recognized.

 B Choose the letter that has the same meaning as the boldfaced expression.

(a) make a decision	(b) remember to consider	(c) forget

1. I haven't **made up my mind** yet. But I was thinking about continuing my studies here through the doctoral program. _____

2. "Did you turn in your application yet?"
   "Oh, it completely **slipped my mind**! I need to do that soon." _____

3. You should **bear in mind** that you only have one year left until graduation. _____

(d) be useful	(e) watch carefully	(f) submit	(g) think about

4. "Have you thought about the type of career you want?"
   "Well, the possibility of working at a company did **cross my mind**." _____

5. You should **keep an eye on** the deadline. You can't miss this opportunity. _____

6. This website should **come in handy**. I recommend you use it. _____

7. Make sure to **hand in** all of the appropriate paperwork on time. _____

 C Read the dialogue with a partner. Individually answer the questions and then compare your answers together.

Lin : Hey, Ken! What's up?

Ken : Hey, Lin! Nothing much. What have you been up to?

Lin : I've actually been thinking a lot recently about my career after graduation. Do you have any plans?

Ken : I'll probably work for a company abroad. How about you?

Lin : Well, I haven't made up my mind yet, but I was thinking about continuing my studies here through the doctoral program.

Ken : Oh, then would you like to become a researcher at a university?

Lin : Well, that was my original plan when I decided to come to this university. But the possibility of working at a company in Japan after receiving my master's degree did cross my mind.

Ken : Well, if you are interested in the corporate world, some companies will be unofficially starting their recruiting activities soon.

Lin : Oh, it completely slipped my mind. Thank you for reminding me.

Ken : Sure. You should keep an eye on the recruiting schedule of each company you are interested in and make sure to attend the career seminars. Also, you'll need to hand in the appropriate application materials on time to go through the selection screening. It's quite an intense process. But bear in mind that you can do almost all of the paperwork online.

Lin : That's a pretty strict recruiting system. If all of that work is imposed on me in addition to my classes and lab work, then I'm not sure if I can do everything. I'll have to consider my options and make a decision soon.

Ken : Don't worry. There are several websites that offer tips on how to survive job hunting in Japan. Here, let me show you my favorite one. It should come in handy. I recommend you check it out sometime. By the way, I'm curious about how students look for jobs in your country.

Lin : Well, compared to Japan, the system is neither well-organized nor strict. Our job market is more flexible in that some students find a job before graduation, while others look for a job afterward. Also, it's common for students to first start working as interns.

Ken : Yeah, internships are actually now becoming increasingly common in Japan.

1. What career options is Lin considering after graduation?

2. Why is Lin undecided about pursuing a job in Japan?

3. How is the recruiting system in Japan different from that of Lin's country?

Discuss the following questions with a partner.

1. What is your plan after graduation? Do you want to work for a company? Or do you want to continue studying at a university?
2. Which do you think is better, the Japanese system or Lin's country's system? Why?
3. What type of working environment would you enjoy? Why?

BACKGROUND SEARCHING
BASICS OF POLYMERS

> While searching for an internship, Ken looked up some companies that engineer materials.

  Learn about the similarities and differences among materials. Listen to the audio and complete the table.

Use the symbols:	+ good	△ neutral	– poor

	Polymers	Metals	Ceramics
Lightweight	+	1. _____	△
Shock-proof	2. _____	+	–
Easy to process	+	+	3. _____
Heat-proof	–	4. _____	+
Thermal conductivity	5. _____	+	△
Deterioration resistance	–	△	6. _____
Electric conductivity	7. _____	+	–

Discuss the following with a partner while referring to the properties of polymers in $\mathcal{A}$.

1. Consider the advantages and disadvantages in $\mathcal{A}$ and write down three products that would benefit from being made out of polymers.
2. Take turns explaining to your partner why using polymers is the best option for each product.

 Read the following explanation about polymers and choose the appropriate words.

Compounds are substances formed from two or more elements that are chemically bonded together. They are made up of several **1.** (molecules / atoms), and each of them contains just a few **2.** (molecules / atoms). Polymers are compounds, meaning they have several elements that are chemically bonded. A distinctive feature of polymers is that they are made of long and repeating chains of molecules which contain an extraordinary number of atoms. Rubber is made from latex, a milky liquid obtained from rubber trees, and is therefore considered a **3.** (natural / synthetic) polymer. In contrast, most of the polymers utilized in industries are synthetic. Therefore, the word 'plastic' is generally used to refer to **4.** (natural / synthetic) polymers.

Synthetic polymers can be divided into two main groups: thermoplastics and thermosetting plastics. Thermoplastics are plastic materials that **5.** (melt / set) by heat into a soft shape and **6.** (melt / set) to form a solid material. This process can be completed as many times as needed using preshaped containers called molds.

Some examples of thermoplastics are as follows:
→ ABS (acrylonitrile butadiene styrene) is stiff and light and is often used in vehicle bodywork.
→ PC (polycarbonate) is used to make strong and **7.** (transparent / opaque) products such as clear panels and see-through vehicle lights.
→ PVC (polyvinyl chloride) is a cheaper plastic used for window frames.

Thermosetting plastics, also called thermosets, are plastic materials that can be heated and molded like thermoplastics. But they do not have recyclability. When cooling during the molding process, a chemical reaction takes place, causing the thermosets to **8.** (soften / cure). This means that thermosets set **9.** (temporarily / permanently) and can never be melted or molded again.

> Examples of thermosets are as follows:
> → Epoxy resins are used in exceptionally strong adhesives.
> → Polyimides are strong and flexible materials used as insulators in some electric cables.

There is another group of polymers called elastomers. Elastomers such as rubber are very **10.** (plastic / elastic), meaning they can be stretched to at least twice their original length when force is applied and can return to their original length when the force is removed.

FINDING AN INTERNSHIP TO JOIN

> After doing some background searching, Ken became interested in a specific type of polymer.

 Learn the basics of biomass. Read the following and fill in the blanks with the words in the top box. Some words need to be modified.

consume	derive	finite	neutral	substitute

Biomass is an organic material, meaning it is **1.** _____ from living organisms such as plants or animals. It is considered a renewable source of energy for heating and electricity.

> → Heat: Wood residue or agricultural waste such as wheat straw are **combusted** and the heat acquired is used for cooking or warming buildings.
> → Electricity: The heat acquired through the combustion is also utilized to produce high-pressure steam. The steam drives turbines to generate electricity.

Renewable biomass such as plants and wood can be easily replaced in the short term. In contrast, fossil fuels such as coal, oil, and natural gas that originate from organic matter, including biomass, are not renewable. This means that they are a **2.** _____

resource. As fossil fuels require millions of years to be created, the existing ones will be depleted far faster than new ones can be made. Biomass is used to produce biofuels, which are expected to be **3.** _____ for fossil fuels. This includes biogas and bioethanol.

→ Biogas: Biogas is methane produced from waste such as food waste or sewage that is used to generate heat or electricity.

→ Bioethanol: Bioethanol is the ethanol produced from crops such as corn or sugarcane through **fermentation** and is used as a gasoline additive to power cars.

Biomass energy is considered to be clean and eco-friendly. When plants are burned, carbon dioxide is emitted. Nonetheless, the emissions are offset when plants grow and **4.** _____ the carbon dioxide through a process called **photosynthesis**. This carbon **5.** _____ nature of biomass energy production is expected to reduce greenhouse gas emissions and thus be one of the solutions to combat climate change. Biomass is also used as raw materials for industrial products such as bioplastics.

→ Bioplastics: Bioplastics are fermented starch extracted from crops such as corn and sugarcane that are used to produce a thermoplastic polymer, polylactic acid, or polylactide (PLA). They are used for food packaging and medical implants. Some bioplastics are biodegradable, meaning that they can **decompose** within months in certain conditions, which is far faster than conventional plastics.

B Refer to the boldfaced vocabulary in **A** and choose the appropriate definition.

1. combustion: _____
(a) the process by which organic material is broken down into smaller constituents

2. fermentation: _____
(b) the process or reaction between a fuel (hydrocarbon) and oxygen to release energy in the form of heat and light

3. photosynthesis: _____
(c) the process by which plants use light energy to synthesize carbohydrates from water and carbon dioxide

4. decomposition: _____
(d) the process in which a microorganism converts sugar into alcohol, gas, or acid

C Ken found a company in Germany that's seeking interns. Listen to the explanation while looking at the figure. Complete Ken's notes with the words in the box.

https://www.polyex.com

Polymer Excellence Corporation

Announcement

We are now recruiting engineering students for an internship in Munich!

About Us

As a compounding company, the mission of Polymer Excellence is to operate manufacturing with new technologies and high-quality management, to satisfy our clients with safe and secure products, and to protect and improve the environment with eco-friendly products.

Our New Products

We are developing green plastics, which are derived from renewable resources and are also biodegradable.

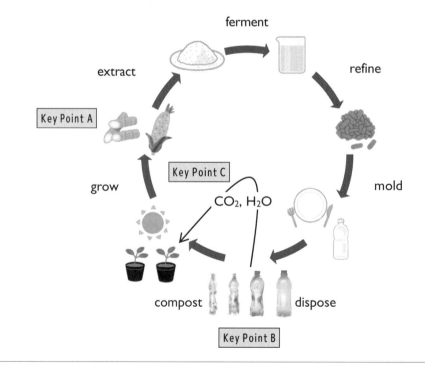

| compost | dependence | durability | exhaustible | net | offset |

Ken's notes

Through its products, Polymer Excellence addresses three environmental issues:

Key Point A   **Breaking away from the 1._____ on fossil fuels**

Most of the currently-used plastic products are petroleum-based; fossil fuels are **2.**_____ resources.

⇒ We need to shift to renewable resources.

Key Point B   **Reducing plastic waste**

Due to their **3.**_____, disposed plastic products and their debris cause serious plastic pollution problems to marine environments.

⇒ Biodegradable plastics can decompose into **4.**_____ within a short time.

Key Point C   **Reducing greenhouse gas emissions**

The emission of carbon dioxide leads to global warming.

⇒ We need to achieve **5.**_____-zero carbon dioxide emissions where CO_2 emitted by composted plastic is **6.**_____ by CO_2 absorbed by plants (carbon neutrality).

PREPARING FOR AN INTERNSHIP

Ken has decided to apply for the internship at Polymer Excellence.

Read the internship application guidelines and circle True or False.

Internship Application Guidelines

Purpose of the Internship

Successful applicants will receive the opportunity to learn about our work and make their own contributions. Interns will be given a variety of tasks and responsibilities that develop their capabilities and provide important experience in a challenging environment. Therefore, skilled and motivated applicants with technical backgrounds are encouraged to apply.

Requirements

We are looking for individuals who are hard-working, positive, open-minded, and willing to learn. Applicants should have at least an undergraduate degree (in engineering or science) or **equivalent**; a master's degree is desired. Applicants should have an intermediate command of English, both written and spoken, as well as possess strong interpersonal and communication skills. While the internship program is open to all students, we want to maintain a broad range of diversity by prioritizing applicants **residing** outside of Europe. Each year we expect to take on between two to three interns.

Time Commitment

The internship generally lasts 3-6 months or longer upon **mutual** agreement.

Conditions

The internship is on a **voluntary** basis, and the contract may be terminated at any time. This is an unpaid internship. However, travel expenses will be **reimbursed**, and daily meals will be provided. The company **assumes** no liability for medical or personal expenses unrelated to the program.

Application Procedure

Please send a cover letter outlining your motivation for applying with an attached resume, as well as a short essay on what you hope to achieve during the program. Be sure to specify your main skills and research interests in relation to the program.

154

1. Interns will focus on doing one particular task.

   [True / False]

2. Students that do not hold a master's degree cannot apply for the internship.

   [True / False]

3. Both engineering and science students are eligible to apply.

   [True / False]

4. Applicants from certain regions are more likely to be chosen than others.

   [True / False]

5. The period of the internship will automatically be increased if the intern submits a request to extend the contract end date.

   [True / False]

6. Travel costs for the internship will be paid for by the company.

   [True / False]

 Review the boldfaced words used in *A* and draw lines to similar words and then lines to opposite words.

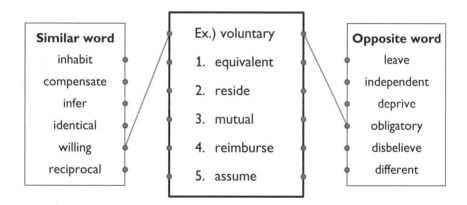

Similar word	Ex.) voluntary	Opposite word
inhabit	1. equivalent	leave
compensate	2. reside	independent
infer	3. mutual	deprive
identical	4. reimburse	obligatory
willing	5. assume	disbelieve
reciprocal		different

C Listen to the conversation and fill in the blanks. The first part of the conversation refers to the left side, and the second refers to the right side.

Ken Nakamura

Master's student

Division of Management of Technology, Graduate School of Engineering, Osaka Tech University, Japan

Email: knakamura@ot.ac.jp   Phone: 81-90-1234-XXX

Education

▷ B.A. in 1. _____

Naniwa Institute of Technology

Research Projects

▷ 2. _____ fulfillment centers

▷ Engineering applications of Material X

Technical Skills

▷ Analysis of technology management

▷ 3. _____ of Material X with tensile strength testing

Conferences and Programs

▷ Poster presentation at the 10th Asian Conference on Materials Science and Engineering in Singapore

▷ 4. _____ program to the United States

Skills

▷ Presentations   5. ☐ ☐ ☐ ☐ ☐

▷ Active Listening   ■ ■ ■ ■ ■

▷ 6. _____   ■ ■ ■ ■ ■

▷ Creativity   7. ☐ ☐ ☐ ☐ ☐

▷ Problem-solving   ■ ■ ■ ■ ☐

Languages

▷ Japanese   ■ ■ ■ ■ ■
(native speaker)

▷ English   8. ☐ ☐ ☐ ☐ ☐
(9. Score: _____)

▷ German   ■ ☐ ☐ ☐ ☐

156

JOB INTERVIEW

After sending the application materials, Ken received an email stating that he has successfully passed the initial screening process!

 Ken needs to prepare for the interview. Finish his prepared responses by choosing the appropriate letters.

Interviewer		Ken's Prepared Answer
1.	Good morning. My name is George Simmel. Please call me George. I work in the Human Resources department.	⇒	It's nice to meet you, George. I'm Ken Nakamura from Osaka Tech University. ____
2.	Could you tell me a little bit about your research?	⇒	My major is Management of Technology, and I belong to the Graduate School of Engineering. ____
3.	Please explain why you applied for this internship.	⇒	I have some international experience that motivated me to work in a different country. ____
4.	What do you think your strengths are?	⇒	I think one of my top skills is teamwork. ____
5.	Where do you see yourself in five years?	⇒	I'm actually hoping that this internship will provide me with guidance on what type of career I want to pursue. ____
6.	Well, that's all the questions I have for you. We will inform you of the results by email within two weeks. Thank you for coming.	⇒	Thank you, George, for your time. ____

(a) Specifically, I volunteered to take care of an international student at our lab, joined a short-term program in the United States, and gave a presentation at an international conference.

(b) Right now, I am studying how to make fulfillment centers more autonomous with robot technologies.

(c) I'm looking forward to hearing from you. Goodbye.

(d) While I haven't exactly figured out what I want to do in the future, I desire to collaborate with others worldwide to produce new and innovative products.

(e) I work with a wide variety of students in my lab from several different countries. Therefore, I have learned how to work well with people from different backgrounds.

(f) I want to thank you for giving me this opportunity.

B Fill in the resume with your information. Then take turns interviewing your partner. Refer to the expressions in **A** for help.

Name:	
Affiliation:	

Education

Research Projects

Technical Skills

Conferences and Programs

Skills
▷ Presentations ☐ ☐ ☐ ☐ ☐
▷ Active Listening ☐ ☐ ☐ ☐ ☐
▷ Teamwork ☐ ☐ ☐ ☐ ☐
▷ Creativity ☐ ☐ ☐ ☐ ☐
▷ Problem-solving ☐ ☐ ☐ ☐ ☐

Languages
▷ _____ ☐ ☐ ☐ ☐ ☐
( )
▷ _____ ☐ ☐ ☐ ☐ ☐
( )
▷ _____ ☐ ☐ ☐ ☐ ☐
( )

Listen to Ken's webcam interview and select the correct answer/s. There may be more than one answer.

1. Which of the following is/are INCORRECT about Ken's self-introduction?
    (a) He didn't major in engineering when he was an undergraduate.
    (b) He is more interested in engineering than management.
    (c) His research concerns the application of robot technologies.

2. Which of the following is/are correct about Ken's explanation of his research?
    (a) His research can contribute to the company's research and development.
    (b) His research focuses on how to enhance efficiency in supply chains.
    (c) He tries to design his research in a way that doesn't harm the environment.

3. Which is/are correct about Ken's motivation to apply for the internship?
    (a) He became interested in international internships through his experience.
    (b) He is determined to work abroad after graduation.
    (c) He wants to work worldwide to produce innovative and environmentally-friendly products.

4. Which is/are INCORRECT about Ken's explanation of his English ability?
    (a) He needs to take an English exam again to meet the internship criteria.
    (b) He's worried that he'll have communication issues during the internship.
    (c) His strength in teamwork can make up for his lack of English ability.

Good news! Ken was accepted into the program. It's time for him to start a new beginning in Germany. Wish him luck!

Unit 1 **LISTENING SCRIPT**

INTRODUCTION: LET'S MEET KEN

A-B (CD-1)

Meet Ken Nakamura. He is from Japan and is a first-year master's student at Osaka Tech University. Ken's major is Management of Technology, or MOT. Are you familiar with this field? It's a fairly new type of study that combines the business features that are useful within a company with technical knowledge. Additionally, Ken is eager to learn about subjects beyond his research focus to broaden his knowledge.

When Ken is not studying, he really enjoys traveling. However, besides going to Guam as a child, he hasn't traveled outside of Japan. He hopes to someday travel abroad to different countries, and so he's motivated to improve his English skills so that he can communicate with people from different backgrounds.

By the way, an international student from Singapore will be joining Ken's lab next week. He'll be studying in Japan for six months as part of an exchange program. Ken is looking forward to meeting him and has already volunteered to show him around the campus and help him get accustomed to life in Japan.

In this first unit, we'll learn about designing and modeling, which are fundamental steps in creating any new products. Given Ken's major and future interests, he will need to learn them as part of his curriculum.

EMAIL EXCHANGE

C (CD-2)

1. Q: Can you show me where the library is?
   a) It is still open.
   b) Yes, please tell me where it is.
   c) Sure, I'd be happy to help you.
2. Q: May I ask who you are?
   a) Yes, allow me to introduce myself.
   b) Alright, please tell me who you are.
   c) Yes, I might be that person.
3. Q: I hope to see you again someday.
   a) I look forward to it.
   b) That was yesterday.
   c) It's the next day.
4. Q: Was there something you wanted to ask me?
   a) Yes, I was wondering if you'd help me.
   b) Yes, go ahead and ask me.
   c) It's about three O'clock now.

MEETING THE EXCHANGE STUDENT

A (CD-3)

John : Hi, sorry. I'm a little lost. I'm not sure if I'm in the right area, but I'm trying to figure out where Building A1 is.

Ken : Actually, this is A1. Hi, I'm Ken. And you are?

John : You're Ken? I'm John from Singapore. We previously chatted through email.

Ken : Oh, hi, John. It's nice to meet you. I'm glad you found the building OK. So, how was your flight? I hope it wasn't too long.

John : Not at all. I just watched a couple of movies to pass the time.

Ken : That's good to hear. Well, as we discussed in our emails, since we'll be lab mates for the duration of your stay in Japan, please let me know if you have any issues or questions. I'm happy to help you out with anything you need.

John : That's very nice of you, Ken. Yes, I will be sure to let you know if I need anything. Oh, here. I brought you some sweets from my country. I hope you like chocolate.

Ken : Oh, you shouldn't have! Thank you! By the way, would you be interested in participating in an upcoming competition? I'm looking for a partner. Here, take a look at this flyer for the event.

John: Design Concept Competition? What type of competition is it?

Ken : I can tell you all about it. But first, I'd like to show you around campus. We can discuss it on the way if that's OK with you.

John: Sure. That sounds good.

Ken : Great. Please follow me.

B (CD-4)

1. I was wondering if you could help me. I'm trying to figure out where Building A1 is.

2. I volunteered to help you out, so let me know if there's anything you need.

3. I'd like to show you around campus if that's OK with you.

4. Would you be interested in participating in a competition?

KEN'S RESEARCH

B (CD-5)

Management of Technology is, just like the name implies, the study of both business and engineering competencies. Many students who have pursued an undergraduate degree in engineering want to also obtain business skills as well such as marketing, accounting, finance, management, and entrepreneurship. Therefore, Management of Technology complements technical knowledge with business features.

C (CD-6)

Fulfillment centers are enormous buildings that store and ship products for online merchants. Merchants send their products to fulfillment centers, and the centers take care of managing the inventories, storage, and distribution to the customers. Modern fulfillment centers apply various state-of-the-art technologies and robots to streamline everything.

The process first starts when a customer places an online order to purchase a product. A robot then receives an instruction to locate the merchandise within the storage shelves. The robot carries the merchandise on wheels to a sorting area. Next, employees gather the merchandise together and pack them into appropriate-sized boxes and send them down a conveyor belt. There, the boxes pass through a sorting machine that identifies, stamps, and directs them where to go. At the end of the conveyor belt, an employee stacks several of the boxes in a large pile and tightly wraps them together in plastic for shipping. Another employee then loads these pallets onto outgoing trucks with a forklift, and the merchandise is ready to be distributed.

Additionally, fulfillment centers are constantly restocking their shelves. When incoming delivery trucks arrive, a forklift driver brings the merchandise to the storage shelves. Now, the whole process is ready to start again.

Unit 2 LISTENING SCRIPT

INTRODUCTION: WORKING IN A LAB

A (CD-7)

In this unit, Ken will help John get accustomed to his new lab. Alongside this, Ken will also learn about static and dynamic principles, which are related to John's physics major. Specifically, he'll learn about different types of forces that push against immobile objects like bridges as they try to bear loads. He'll also learn about the forces that push against moving objects like rockets, drones, and planes. It sounds like a lot of fun! Nevertheless, in order to ensure that John can conduct experiments in the lab, Ken must first help him gain sufficient knowledge about the rules, regulations, and safety procedures. Of course, Ken is looking forward to helping John out in this regard.

B (CD-8)

Let's learn about three types of bodies. The word *body* here just means an *object* or *thing*. Therefore, we are just talking about different types of objects.

First, we have rigid bodies. The word *rigid* means *hard*. So, a rigid body just means a *hard object*. A rigid body is something that is solid and is supposed to stay the same without bending or stretching. Nevertheless, if enough force is put on it, it will break, meaning it won't return to its natural shape afterwards, even if you stop putting force on it.

Next, there are deformable bodies. The word *deformable* simply means *able to be deformed*, or *able to change*. What kind of object do you think is a deformable body? Well, it is anything that can bend without breaking. A deformable body is the opposite of a rigid body. If you put force on it, it can bend and change its structure. And when you let go of the force, it can return to its original form.

Finally, we have fluid bodies. *Fluid* just means *liquid*, or something that is in a wet state. Unlike solid bodies, fluid bodies move like water. But keep in mind that rigid and deformable bodies can both be melted into a fluid body if enough heat is applied, even metal or rubber.

D (CD-9)

Imagine a support beam for a house like the picture on the left. The purpose of the beam is to hold the house up and support the weight of the walls and roof; it must bear a load. To *bear something* means to hold its weight. And a *load* is just an object that is being carried. But the building is very heavy, and it puts substantial weight onto the support beam. If there is too much weight, the support beam will bend or even break. The force that pushes on an object that is not in motion is called static force. The support beam must balance this force while remaining still.

Now imagine a rocket flying in the air like the picture on the left. Unlike the house support beam, this rocket is moving fast. While it's in motion, there is a force pushing against it. The force that pushes against a moving object is called dynamic force. As you can imagine, more parameters are needed to calculate where the rocket will travel. Such parameters include velocity, which measures how fast something is moving in a certain direction. There's also acceleration, the increase in speed within a certain amount of time. We also need to measure the resistance that an object has when rubbing against another object, which is known as friction.

Now, while the support beam and rocket have different forces acting on them, they are both considered rigid bodies. This means that they are not supposed to bend, break, or melt when forces push against them.

SAFETY PROCEDURES IN THE LAB

B (CD-10)

Professor: Good morning, class. I'm sure you're all excited to start your experiments, but there are a few things that I have to go over first before we proceed. So, let's now talk about the list of things that you need to bring to the lab next week. First, everyone needs to bring shoes that have closed toes, meaning that your feet and toes cannot be exposed. Things like sandals are prohibited, so you can't bring them.

John: Do we need to purchase steel-toed boots?

Professor: OK, good question. For those who don't know, steel-toed boots are boots that have steel plates protecting the toes from heavy or sharp objects. They are quite useful as a safety precaution when visiting construction sites. Nevertheless, they won't be mandatory in this lab. Next, you'll be needing a lab coat, along with safety goggles. You can find these at the university store on campus for a decent price. Now, the lab is equipped with a state-of-the-art ventilation system to air-out any toxic chemicals. Hence, you will not require a respirator mask. However, there is still the possibility of an emergency, and in that case, such masks will be available. Finally, in principle, vinyl gloves will be given to students at no cost. However, please keep in mind that our supply is limited. Depending on certain circumstances, we may ask students to start purchasing gloves if there are too many being wasted. Alright, I'll now pass out the lab safety rules. Make sure to read this before next week's class.

D (CD-11)

John: Hey Ken, do you have a minute?

Ken : Sure, John, what's going on?

John: Well, I've been reading the lab rules that the professor gave us, and they're kind of confusing and unclear. I don't think I sufficiently understand them. Could you help clarify a few things for me?

Ken : Yeah, sure. Which parts were you having trouble understanding?

John: For example, the part regarding no food in the lab. What about water? Can I bring a water bottle?

Ken : Actually, no. The professor established a rule last year, banning all drinks after a student spilled his soda.

John: Oh, I see. OK. And what about the part regarding wearing accessories while conducting experiments? So, I'm not allowed to wear a watch, right?

Ken : The professor was mostly talking about things like earrings and other jewelry. But keep in mind that you still need to keep track of time, so don't worry. I don't think that would constitute a prohibited item.

John: That's good. And the rules said no sandals, right? But what about these? [points to his feet]

Ken : Anything that has exposed toes is dangerous. I think yours fall in that category, unfortunately.

John: OK, I understand. Oh, what about hair caps? I think some labs require those back in my country.

Ken : Students only need to tie up or cover their hair if it is long. You should be fine, though.

John: Alright, I understand. There's a lot to remember, and it seems like I have a great potential to make mistakes.

Ken : Don't worry. The professor is mostly just trying to ensure that you're not putting yourself in danger.

A WELCOME DINNER FOR THE NEW LAB MEMBERS

C (CD-12)

1. Is there a way for me to get ahold of you?
   (a) Yes, I can.
   (b) Sure, I'll hold on.
   (c) Yeah, you can reach me on my phone.
2. Do you want to meet sometime?
   (a) Sure, let me give you my contact information.
   (b) The time is now eight O'clock.
   (c) Yes, I sometimes meet you.
3. Which approach did you take?

(a) I just followed the directions in the book.

(b) I didn't take anything.

(c) It took me a long time.

4. Feel free to stop by any time after 6 pm.

(a) OK, I'll come by around that time.

(b) Don't worry. We'll finish it before that time.

(c) So, why can't I come?

5. Was there anything else you wanted to discuss with me?

(a) No, let's talk about it right now.

(b) No, that's about it. I'll talk to you later.

(c) Sure, what do you want to talk about?

Unit 3 LISTENING SCRIPT

INTRODUCTION: APPLYING FOR A STUDY ABROAD PROGRAM

A (CD-13)

After talking with John about his country, different cultures, and the world, Ken started to become interested in studying abroad. In this unit, he will decide to apply for a three-week study abroad program at Rocklin University in the United States starting from August 1st. There, Ken is looking forward to participating in many activities such as attending a seminar on business and electricity innovations, improving his English ability, and even conducting some research if he has the chance. However, his main study abroad purpose will be to put himself into a different culture to broaden his perspective. He is a little nervous about the program, though. For instance, he is worried that he might not be able to communicate well with his host family,

or he may fail to understand what his teachers say in class. But, setting these fears aside, Ken is overall very excited to begin this adventure!

ATTENDING A SEMINAR: THE WORLD-FAMOUS INVENTOR

D (CD-14)

1. I find out what the world needs. Then I go ahead and invent it.

2. I have not failed. I've just found 10,000 ways that won't work.

3. Many of life's failures are people who did not realize how close they were to success when they gave up.

4. Just because something doesn't do what you planned it to do doesn't mean it's useless.

WATCHING THE NEWS ABOUT ELECTRIC CARS

A (CD-15)

Reporter:

Good evening. In today's business news, automobile company Roger stated that they are allocating an estimated $400 million towards pursuing their goal of creating efficient electric vehicles within three years. An electric vehicle, or EV, is an automobile that uses an electric motor as its primary source of propulsion. The electrical energy for these motors is stored in rechargeable batteries. One of the primary benefits of an EV is the lack of CO_2 emissions. To investigate further, we collected data on various countries' supply and demand for electric cars. [...]

C (CD-16)

Host Father: Would you like to buy an electric car in the near future?

Ken : Hmm... It depends on the price. In my

opinion, they are still too expensive despite their efficiency.

Host Father: I know what you mean. Oh, speaking of the price of electric cars, I read a news article online that was mentioning how the batteries for electric cars will be getting much cheaper in the near future.

Ken : That would be great.

Host Father: Right now, you can see electric cars here and there. But I believe we'll soon see them everywhere.

Ken : I would be happy if that happened since electric cars are relatively environmentally friendly.

Host Father: I agree with you. But I'm sure there are both pros and cons of driving electric vehicles, don't you think?

Ken : Well, the downside is that with the technology right now, the distance you can drive on a single charge is somewhat limited.

Host Father: Yeah, that's definitely a factor to consider. And what about the benefits?

Ken : Let's see… From what I know, it will always be cheaper overall, right?

Host Father: I doubt it. But it really depends on how many miles you put on the car and how long you keep it. If you don't drive much and end up selling the car in a couple of years, then a gas-powered car might be cheaper in the end.

Ken : That's true.

D (CD-17)

1. In my opinion, they are still too expensive.
2. I believe we'll soon see them everywhere.
3. I agree with you. But I'm sure there are both pros and cons, don't you think?
4. Yeah, that's definitely a factor to consider.
5. From what I know, it will always be cheaper overall, right?
6. I doubt it.

INTRODUCTION: SENDING AN EMAIL TO A PROFESSOR

A (CD-18)

Ken has decided to visit a laboratory at Rocklin University during his stay in the United States. One of the reasons why he chose to study at this university was because he wants to meet Professor Brown, who has world fame. The professor manages a laboratory at the university called the Future Energy Lab. A few months ago, Ken saw Professor Brown give a presentation on TV about the importance of researching future energy such as renewable and clean energy for a sustainable future. Professor Brown also emphasized not just doing research, but also cooperating with companies to benefit society. This idea is closely related to Ken's research field of Management of Technology that considers the combination of research and business. If possible, he would like to visit the laboratory in mid-August before he goes back to Japan.

VISITING PROFESSOR BROWN'S LAB: MEETING A STUDENT

A (CD-19)

Ken : Nice to meet you. I'm Ken Nakamura. Please call me Ken. I'm very excited to visit Professor Brown's lab today.

Kate: Hi Ken, It's nice to meet you, too. My name's Kate. I'm a Ph.D. student at this lab, and I'll be in charge of giving you a tour today.

Ken : Great, thank you so much. To be honest, Kate, I'm a little nervous.

Kate: Oh, don't worry, you can take it easy.

Everyone here is very friendly and happy to have guests. Actually, I just came back from Osaka. I attended a conference there. Japan was amazing.

Ken : No way! I am from Osaka too.

Kate: Really? How interesting! I want to talk to you more about that later. But for now, let's get started on the tour. If you'd like, I'll first show you the main facilities.

Ken : That sounds good. Thank you again for taking time to do this for me today.

Kate: It's my pleasure. Please follow me.

Unit 5 LISTENING SCRIPT

INTRODUCTION: ATTENDING A WORKSHOP

A (CD-20)

Ken has now returned to Japan after his stay in the U.S. where he enjoyed having various discussions about global topics and meeting new people from different backgrounds. He now wants to find another opportunity to increase his knowledge. In this unit, Ken will happen to find a workshop about future technology. It will be held on August 30th with 15 different related topics. Ken's reasoning for joining the workshop is that, in order to participate in the international community, he believes he must develop a strong, broad network beyond his research field. Of course, he could also improve his English communication by participating in discussion sessions throughout the workshop. His only concern about the workshop is that he doesn't have much background in the computer-

related field. Overall, he'll need to make sure to brush up on both his English proficiency and related knowledge.

DISCUSSION: ARTIFICIAL INTELLIGENCE PREDICTIONS

B (CD-21)

1. There are some who predict that AI will cause people's intelligence to diminish.
2. On the other hand, others think that the utilization of AI is justified.
3. Those that think that they don't need AI for recruiting purposes at all exceeded half of the participants.
4. The AI systems were precise more than 80% of the time.
5. Many people are debating the implications of relying on AI, as it continues to rapidly exceed our expectations.

C (CD-22)

Ken : Let's take a look at the graph they surveyed before the workshop starts.

John: Alright, let's see. It looks like 43% of people in their 30s think that people's ability to use their brains will diminish because of AI, while only 25% of people in their 20s think that way.

Ken : That's interesting. Also, look at the second question. 40% of people in their 30s think that AI will pose a danger in the future, while just 20% of people in their 20s think so. This means that almost half of the people in their 30s think that it'll be dangerous. I wonder why.

John: Hmm… maybe the younger generation is more accustomed to technology, and so they think that the utilization of AI is more justified.

Ken : That makes sense. That's probably why 10% of people in their 30s also worry about AI, while only 5% of those in their 20s think that way.

John: Yeah, but look at the last question. Among the people in their 30s, 73% think AI will make life more convenient.

Ken : However, people in their 20s answered even higher than that at 82%, meaning almost all of the younger generation people think AI will make our lives more convenient.

D (CD-23)

Ken : How about we move on to the survey question, "If AI was in charge of the recruiting process, how would you feel about it?"?

John: Sure. I thought the result was interesting. The people who think that they don't need AI for recruiting at all exceeded half... 55% to be precise.

Ken : I was surprised by the result too. I heard that many companies are already partially using AI for the initial steps of their recruiting processes. But only 13% of the people surveyed here answered that they don't mind if AI is partially used for the recruiting process.

John: Yeah. And what's more interesting is that, while 55% of people are against using AI, 32% of people are fine with using AI for the entire recruiting process.

Ken : How interesting!

E (CD-24)

Ken : Let's take a look at the next graph on jobs that might disappear by AI versus jobs that will survive.

John: Wow, the number one job that might be taken over is telephone operators at 99%.

Ken : True. And it's the same with data inputters, which is 99% as well.

John: This means they'll pretty much be gone. Also, taxi drivers have a high chance of disappearing since the percentage is 89%. And on the opposite end, people in the medical field, which includes doctors, just have a 0.4% chance of losing their jobs to AI.

Ken : Software engineers have a 4.2% chance, which is pretty low. I would imagine this is because we need people to create the AI software. I wonder if that number will increase in the future.

John: Yeah, maybe. Imagine how you'd feel if you were designing the same program that will take your job!

PRESENTATION: ARTIFICIAL INTELLIGENCE PREDICTIONS

A (CD-25)

1. I appreciate this opportunity to present my research to you today.
2. I am going to give a presentation regarding the topic of "What will our future be like with AI?".
3. Now, let me begin by outlining my presentation.
4. I will begin by providing background information on AI.
5. Then I will introduce two opposite opinions.
6. Finally, I will describe how the future world would be like with AI.
7. Now, let me summarize my presentation.
8. I would like to emphasize that there are two opposite sides to the debate.

Unit 6 LISTENING SCRIPT

INTRODUCTION: THE BACKGROUND OF A COMPETITION

A (CD-26)

In this unit, Ken, John and their classmate Lin will learn about an upcoming engineering competition where a number of universities will participate in constructing and piloting an aircraft that can fly the farthest. After reading the details, they'll become interested in competing. However, to achieve such a task, they must first learn about the aspects of measurements and mechanisms; accurate measurements are required to construct a flying device, and various mechanisms are involved in operating it. Ken also needs to be able to cooperate with his partners using English and therefore needs to be able to use relevant expressions and vocabulary while communicating with each other. You may encounter this type of opportunity in your life as well, so pay attention and find out what happens!

AN ADVERTISEMENT FOR AN ENGINEERING COMPETITION

C (CD-27)

Ken : Hey, Lin, how's it going? Are you busy right now?

Lin : Hi, Ken. No, I'm free. What's going on?

Ken : Have you seen this advertisement for an engineering competition? The Shiga local government organizes it. Contestants create an aircraft and compete to see how far they can fly it!

Lin : Oh, no. I haven't heard about it. Do you mind if I take a look?

Ken : Sure.

Lin : This seems pretty interesting. Were you thinking about doing it?

Ken : Yeah, maybe. I think it would be fun. But there are some parts in this advertisement that I don't really understand.

Lin : Which parts?

Ken : Well, for instance, *convening at Lake Biwa*.

Lin : Oh, *convene* just means *to meet* or *join together*. So, the competition location will be at Lake Biwa.

Ken : Oh, I see. Thanks. And what about the part where it explains the judging criteria regarding creative design? I didn't quite understand it.

Lin : It is saying that we must demonstrate, which means show, our capacity to differentiate our team from the rest. So, it just means that we must show our ability to be unique.

Ken : I see. Well, if we place in the top three, we'll receive a scholarship. And I talked to our professor about the event and he said that he'd give extra credit for anyone who competes! Would you be interested in it?

Lin : Hmm, it sounds interesting. But we'd also need more teammates, right? I think this job requires more than two people.

Ken : Actually, I've already talked to John, and he sounded interested. If you and he join, we'd have a three-member team. What do you think?

Lin : I see. Well, can I check my schedule first and follow up with you later?

Ken : Yeah, sure. Just let me know sometime this week if you could.

DOING THE MEASUREMENTS I: DRAWING UP THE BLUEPRINTS

C (CD-28)

This image is a cross section of a passenger aircraft. A cross section is an image that has been cut open in order to be able to examine it as a flat surface. By cutting a section of the aircraft open, we can now easily measure some important dimensions. First, let's talk about the circumference. Notice that the word *circumference* sounds like *circle*. Well, the circumference is just the measurement of the length of the entire outer circle. Now, how about the diameter? The diameter is the length from one end of the outer circle to the opposite point at the other end. It's a straight line drawn all the way through the circle. Next, we have the radius. The radius measures the length between one side of the outer circle to the center of the circle. Lastly, there is an arc. The word *arc* means a shape that bends. It is one part of a circle, meaning that it is a piece of the circumference.

WORKING TOGETHER TO PLAN THE PROJECT

C (CD-29)

John: Alright. Are you guys ready to talk about coming up with a plan for completing the project on time?

Lin : OK, yeah. Well, I think we need to first decide the design of the aircraft by drawing up the blueprints. We'll need to do that by early September. Let's say by September 4th?

Ken : That sounds good. By the way, do we need to send a rough draft to the professor?

John: That won't be necessary. We just need to send him a final report after the event.

Lin : Alright. Next, when do you think we can complete the measurements?

Ken : How about sometime in October?

Lin : I think that would be a little too late because we wouldn't have time to do the rest of the required steps. I was thinking more like mid-September. How about the 15th?

Ken : I think we can do that.

Lin : OK, that schedule leaves us enough time to acquire the necessary materials. I recommend that we use something light, yet durable. I know it will cost more, but if we use cheap materials, they may end up disqualifying us.

John: I agree. I can be in charge of getting the materials. I'll try to get that done by October 1st.

Ken : Great, thanks, John. And if you are unsure about anything, we can always ask our professor for a second opinion. But for now, I think we are fine. Now, after we obtain the materials, we can begin assembling the aircraft. How long do you think that will take?

John: Well, if we start on October 1st, I don't see any issue with finishing the assembly by October 15th. After that, we can have a whole two weeks to conduct test flights. That should be an adequate amount of time to make sure everything is working. We can be finished with the test flights by November 1st, right in time for the event.

LEARNING ABOUT MECHANISMS

B (CD-30)

There are several mechanisms that we use in our daily lives. Here are three common ones. First, there are gear mechanisms. Gears contain cogs, which are circular wheels with sharp-looking teeth. These teeth interlock with each other so that when one moves, the others move as well. Gear mechanisms are often used in vehicle transmissions and analog clocks.

Next, we have pulley mechanisms. You can just think of the word *pull*. A pulley mechanism consists of a rope that runs through a hanging wheel and is tied to a weighted block. Pulleys are used to transmit tension force to the block. When someone pulls on the rope, they can lift heavier objects with much less effort. Pulleys are often used in elevators and construction cranes.

Finally, there are crank mechanisms. A crank mechanism consists of an arm attached to a rotating shaft at a right angle. A right angle is an angle that is at 90 degrees. When the shaft turns, it makes the crank arm slide back and forth in a linear motion. Crank mechanisms are often used to power the pistons in vehicle engines.

COMPETING IN THE EVENT

B (CD-31)

Ken :

Taking part in the competition was a very interesting experience, but not everything worked out exactly as we had planned. Let me explain the day.

In the early morning, we loaded our aircraft assembly into my mother's van and drove for an hour and a half to the event. We arrived just before eight O'clock, which left us plenty of time to set everything up before our designated time. We were very hungry and decided to eat an early lunch. Afterwards, we were busy doing the necessary preparations. All of a sudden, it was our turn to compete. We pushed our aircraft onto the enormous launch pad and did one final check. Since I was the designated pilot, I nervously climbed onto the top of the plane and held on tight. My teammates pushed me off the ramp as hard as they could and I felt the sensation of flying! It was by far the most exciting feeling I've ever experienced. However, within seconds, a problem became apparent; I could feel the aircraft beginning to break apart! Then I watched in horror as a wing broke off, and I crashed into the water. Later that day, we kept wondering what had gone wrong. In the end, we all came to the conclusion that we had not been as thorough as we should have.

So, it turns out that we shouldn't have cut so many corners! We initially spent too much time making sure everything was perfect. But in the end, we had to skip steps to make sure we could finish in time. As a result, we missed the mark by a lot! But overall, we had a great experience and were awarded a good amount of extra credit from our professor. I think that alone was worth the effort. Well, better luck next time.

Unit 7 LISTENING SCRIPT

INTRODUCTION: TAKING A CLASS

A (CD-32)

To broaden his perspective and understanding of engineering, Ken has decided to take a course in English entitled Introduction to Ocean Engineering and Naval Architecture that is offered outside of his major. While it is not easy for Ken to understand other disciplines not directly related to his own such as fluid and air dynamics, he enjoys studying them nevertheless. One of the reasons why Ken decided to take this course is because the class gets the opportunity to tour a shipyard. Ken has never seen a shipyard before and is very excited to take part in it. However, he will first need to listen carefully to the safety instructions given by the professor. Luckily, Ken's international friend Lin is also taking the class as part of her Ocean Engineering major. Lin often helps Ken whenever he finds the lectures difficult to understand.

B-C (CD-33)

Professor:

We have studied the basic mechanisms and structures of ships so far. Now, while it is important for students to study theories in fluid and air dynamics in the classroom, it is also essential to learn how to put the theories into practice. It is for this purpose that we will be touring a ship manufacturing company.

Seto Shipbuilding Company has several shipyards, all of which face the Seto Inland Sea. One is located in Hiroshima and the others in Ehime. The company also has an office in Tokyo, as well as a European office in Amsterdam. The shipyard that we will visit next week is the newest one and is in charge of the research and development of new technologies for the company. It has three dry docks, one of which is the largest in the company. The shipyard builds a large line-up of ships of all different sizes for various purposes.

PREPARING FOR THE TOUR: SAFETY TIPS

A (CD-34)

Professor:

I will now discuss the safety rules while on the premise of the shipyard. Be sure to follow these rules at all times. I'll start with dress attire. For your safety, please refrain from wearing short-sleeve shirts. Instead, you'll need to wear long-sleeved shirts and trousers. I know it'll be hot outside, but it is important to protect your skin against injury by sharp corners or jagged surfaces. Furthermore, loose or baggy outfits such as flare skirts run the risk of being caught in machinery, so please avoid wearing them. Also, it might be sunny, so you can bring a hat if you'd like. Next, to protect your feet, any type of footwear with exposed toes will be prohibited. This includes sandals and flip-flops. Since we'll be walking around the shipyard for an extended time, we recommend that you bring comfortable walking shoes such as sneakers. Now, I know you probably want to take some photos. This is fine, but please ask the guide for permission first. Lastly, there will be no eating or drinking while on the tour. A light snack will be provided before the tour, and we'll have lunch right after.

THE CLASS TOURS A SHIPYARD

A (CD-35)

The shipbuilding process involves several steps from start to finish. First, ships are designed with the consideration of meeting customers' needs. Frequent consultation with clients is, therefore, important during this stage. The next step is lofting. Lofting is a drafting technique to generate curved lines for streamlined products such as aircraft and ships. Next, based on the model created by lofting, each part of the ship is cut from steel plates using an automated Numerical Control Cutting machine. The materials are then heated and bent into the curvy parts of the ship. After bending, the ship is divided into several separate blocks and assembled in a process called the block construction method. After that, the assembled blocks are installed and joined with the use of a crane. Before the ship can enter the ocean, it must be painted to prevent corrosion. Finally, the ship is ready to be launched into the sea. It sets sail and is delivered to the customer.

LEARNING ABOUT CORPORATE SOCIAL RESPONSIBILITY (CSR)

B (CD-36)

1. Our mission is to build a brighter future not only for our company but also for the whole shipbuilding industry. We are proactively engaged in promoting activities

such as making our industry more appealing to the youth and fostering the careers of maritime specialists who will lead the future of the industry.

2. We are committed to making great contributions to the development and prosperity of local communities while retaining trust and gratitude. By cooperating with local governments and supporting and participating in community events, we are seeking to strengthen our relationship with the people further.

3. Recently, companies are inclined to be increasingly aware of their social responsibility and are altering their business activities to be more eco-friendly. We also endeavor to reduce our impact on the environment and restore nature by utilizing renewable energy and facilitating ecological projects.

Unit 8 LISTENING SCRIPT

INTRODUCTION: PARTICIPATING IN A SPECIAL PROGRAM

A (CD-37)

After the tour to the shipyard, Ken will meet up again with Lin on campus. There, Lin will invite Ken to take part in a special program whereby students can visit various manufacturing companies and take part in a one-day internship. The program is open to students from all technical majors, but in order to participate, Ken must take a lecture on the basics of machining and joining in manufacturing. Afterwards, he will get the opportunity to visit two companies: one that

manufactures special nuts and bolts, and another that produces steel. He will then spend a day at each company working on group projects, gaining real experience, and getting to know the companies. Let's follow along and find out what happens!

B (CD-38)

Ken : Hey, Lin! What's going on?

Lin : Hi, Ken! Nothing much. How have you been since I last saw you? I haven't seen you in a while.

Ken : I've been very busy as usual, attending classes and doing lab work. Oh, and research on top of that.

Lin : I know exactly what you mean! Actually, I'm pretty busy as well. By the way, have you met Luke?

Luke: You must be Ken. Lin told me that she made a new Japanese friend. It's nice to meet you.

Ken : Hi, Luke! It's nice to meet you, too. So, what are you guys up to today?

Lin : We just found out about a special program that offers one-day internships at manufacturing companies. Have you heard about it?

Ken : No, I haven't. But I thought your major was Ocean Engineering.

Lin : Yeah, it is. But it's open to any technical majors. We just have to attend a lecture on manufacturing first before we can take part in it.

Luke: It seems like a great opportunity to learn about the industry and get to experience real companies. Plus, it would look good on our resumes!

Lin : You know what? Ken, why don't you join as well? It'll be fun!

Ken : Oh, I don't know. I'm not sure if I'm up for it. I mean, I'm already so busy and all.

Luke: Well, it's up to you. But it seems like it would be very beneficial if you can make it.

Ken : Yeah, it seems interesting. I'll have to think about it.

ATTENDING A LECTURE: BASICS OF MACHINING

B (CD-39)

Now, let's take a closer look at machining. What exactly does *machining* mean? Well, if you machine something, it means that you use machines to cut some pieces of materials and shape them into components. The pieces you cut are called workpieces. To make holes, grooves, or threads on a workpiece, you'll need special equipment for each purpose. Let's take metals, for example, which, as you probably know, are often machined. If you make a hole in a sheet of metal with a drill, waste will be produced. This waste is referred to as swarf or chips. While machining, we pump a liquid called cutting liquid onto the workpiece to wash away the swarf. Additionally, the drill can quickly heat up due to friction, and the cutting liquid also acts as a coolant that prevents overheating. In manufacturing, machining is usually not guided by humans, but by computers. These are called Computer Numerical Control systems (CNC), or simply Numerical Control systems (NC). We first design the shapes and sizes of components using software such as Computer-Aided Design (CAD) or Computer-Aided Manufacturing (CAM). Then we feed the information into the CNC systems.

LEARNING JOINING TECHNIQUES AT A COMPANY

A (CD-40)

Luke: There are several ways to connect individual components. Roughly speaking, we can divide them into two groups: mechanical joints and non-mechanical joints. Let me draw a 3 by 3 table to show you what I'm talking about. Now, here in the top row, we have two types of joints: mechanical and non-mechanical. Then in the left-side column, I put temporary and permanent. First, do you guys know any examples of mechanical joints?

Lin : I believe one example would be using fasteners such as nuts and bolts.

Luke: That's right. Any other examples?

Ken : How about screws?

Luke: Right. Screws are also fasteners that are mechanical joints. So, do you think the two examples that you guys just mentioned are temporary or permanent joints?

Ken : They seem like temporary joints to me.

Luke: That's exactly right. Now, do you know any examples of permanent mechanical joints?

Lin : Rivets, I think.

Ken : I'm not familiar with rivets. What are they, exactly?

Luke: Well, they look similar to bolts. However, unlike bolts, rivets don't have a threaded body. So, if you want to join two thin plates together with rivets, you need to do more than just pre-drill holes and insert them. After inserting them into the holes, you must flatten one of the ends to make another head. Alright, lastly, how about non-mechanical permanent joints? Any ideas?

Lin : There's welding. That's non-mechanical, and that's certainly a permanent joint. You can't undo that.

Luke: Exactly. And then finally, there are adhesives. Like welding, once an adhesive is applied, it's difficult to remove it.

B (CD-41)

Luke: Hey, Ken! Have you ever heard of Hardlock before?

Ken : You mean like Hard Rock Café?

Luke: No, Hardlock, not rock.

Ken : Ah, Hardlock. Yeah, I've read an online article about their products. Don't they produce parts for trains?

Luke: Yeah. They're mostly known for their nuts and bolts used in bullet trains. Their products are also used in cars, highways, bridges, transmission towers, and ships. Do you know why their products are so unique?

Ken : Well, judging by their company name, I'm guessing their nuts and bolts won't loosen.

Luke: Yeah, that's right. Their key is in using a special wedge. I'm sure you're probably familiar with the Japanese traditional technique of using wedges in wooden architecture.

Ken : Ah, yes, a wedge. Wait a moment. Let me draw a picture. This is what you're talking about, right?

Luke: Exactly. A wedge is a piece of wood that has a triangular shape with one thick edge and one pointed edge. Just like you drew here, when we connect two wooden parts together, we use a mortise and tenon joint. A mortise is a cut into the left side and is designed to receive the tenon. A tenon is the object at the end of the other side and is shaped to fit exactly into the mortise. And when we insert a wedge into the gap between the mortise and tenon, the two parts will tightly connect. So, based on this method, Hardlock uses a similar technique with its products to ensure a tight and secure fit.

VISITING A STEEL COMPANY

A (CD-42)

Tour guide:

Welcome to Kansai Steel Corporation. First, let me roughly outline our company's business activities and then explain our automatic welding system in detail. Please look at the sheet I gave you that lists the categories of our products. Some of the parts are missing. See if you can complete the list while I explain it. As you can see, our company produces products within the categories of iron and steel, welding, aluminum and copper, and machinery. First, our iron and steel products are divided into five categories. This includes wire rods and bars, steel sheets, steel plates, steel forging and castings, and titanium. Next, within the welding business, we offer a wide range of welding products and services that include robots and electric power sources and welding materials. Third, our aluminum and copper business is working to strengthen and expand its distinctive products by positioning the automotive and IT industries as key fields. This business includes aluminum plates and copper sheets and strips. Finally, there is the machinery business, which includes industrial machinery and equipment. This business covers five products: standard compressors, rotating machinery, rolling mills, plastic processing machinery, and ultra high-pressure equipment.

WORKING ON A PROJECT AT THE COMPANY

B (CD-43)

1. The deadline is getting near. We have to make sure that we can follow through on the project.

2. I don't need an answer today. Please think it over and let me know sometime this week.

3. It appears that the work is going well. You're all doing an excellent job.

4. I know you feel like you can't take on more responsibilities at this time. However, I really need your help.

1. This is a lot of responsibility. Can I count on you to complete it on time?
   (a) Yes, I can count the time.
   (b) Yes, I can do it.
   (c) Yes, you can finish it then.

2. Would you like a hand with that?
   (a) I'll turn it in today.
   (b) I'm sorry, but I can't.
   (c) No, thanks. I'm fine.

3. I need you to hold off on ordering the supplies.
   (a) Alright. Just let me know when I can do it.
   (b) OK. I'll finish it as soon as possible.
   (c) How many should I order?

4. Hey, I wanted to touch base with you regarding the task I gave you.
   (a) I understand. It won't happen again.
   (b) OK, have you finished it yet?
   (c) Sure, I have time to talk now.

Unit 9 LISTENING SCRIPT

INTRODUCTION: RECEIVING AN EMAIL FROM JOHN

A (CD-45)

In this unit, Ken will receive an email from John, who has returned to Singapore after his stay in Japan. It turns out that John recently presented his research at a conference in his country. Ken will then realize that he can visit John if he also attends an international conference held in Singapore. With Lin's help, he will find a conference and decide to apply for it. Fortunately, Ken's proposal for a poster presentation will be accepted, and he'll join the conference. There, Ken will meet up with John and give his presentation.

BACKGROUND SEARCHING: FINDING A CONFERENCE TO ATTEND

A (CD-46)

Lin : Hi, Ken, what are you doing? Are you searching for something?

Ken : Hi, Lin. Yeah, I'm actually considering attending an international conference.

Lin : Wow, that's great! Where will you go? The U.S.? Or maybe Europe? I went to Germany last year for a conference, and it was great.

Ken : Well, I'm thinking about meeting John in Singapore. So, I'm interested in conferences in Southeast Asia.

Lin : There's always conferences going on in Indonesia, but that's a bit far. I know, you should look into Malaysia. It's close to Singapore. By the way, what type of conference are you interested in exactly?

Ken : I'm not sure yet, but I guess something related to business and engineering. Do you know how I can look up some information?

Lin : Yeah, there are a lot of websites that post international conferences held all over the world. Just do an internet search. Here, this website lists upcoming international conferences based on country and theme.

Ken : Wow, there are so many! Let's see, chemical engineering, electrical engineering... These have potential.

Lin : There are too many unrelated conferences like business management. Let's filter the results a little bit. OK, how about this one?

Ken : The 10th Asian Conference on Materials Science. Materials science seems interesting. And it will take place in

Singapore too! The dates even match my schedule. Have you heard about it?

Lin : Yeah, actually, I think my professor attended last year. Before deciding on it, I'd recommend consulting with him first.

Ken : That's a good idea. And if it all goes well and my proposal is accepted, I'll need to practice giving a presentation in English!

SIGNING UP FOR A CONFERENCE

B (CD-47)

Lin : Hi, Ken, what are you up to?

Ken : I'm sending the abstract of my paper to the conference. Do you have a minute to help me with some parts that I don't understand? For instance, how should I write my name? Should I put my first name first, followed by my family name? Or maybe my family name in capital letters with a comma and then my first name?

Lin : Usually, Japanese conferences want family names first. But since this is an international one, you'd probably be safe with putting your first name, followed by your family name.

Ken : Got it. Thanks!
Oh, what do I put under *affiliation*?

Lin : Let's see. That would normally be your place of work. But since you're a student, putting *Osaka Tech University* will be fine. Also, maybe your department.

Ken : OK, then I'll put *Graduate School of Engineering* before *Osaka Tech University*. Next up, for the telephone number, can I use the one for the lab? 06-6879-555?

Lin : That's fine. But you probably want to use the international format. Just delete the first zero and replace it with the number eight. By the way, I noticed that you listed your personal email address. I'd recommend using your university

address instead; it will make you look more legitimate.

Ken : OK, so that's *knakamura@ot.ac.jp*. Got it! Thanks. Now the type of presentation. That's easy. That'll be a student poster presentation. It looks like that's it. I'll go ahead and send it now. Thank you for your help!

PREPARING FOR A POSTER PRESENTATION

B (CD-48)

I. If materials are exposed to forces, their shape may change. This is called deformation. We can think about two different types of forces. The first is stretching force, which is known as tension. The second is crushing force called compression. If you stretch a material that doesn't have tensile strength, it will extend or elongate. And if you crush a material and it cannot resist the force, it will deform. This means that it does not have high compressive strength. Keep in mind that the tensile strength of a material is usually lower than the compressive strength.

II. There are two types of deformation of a material. If you stretch a material and it can return to its original shape, it is elastic. A rubber band can be elastically deformed, while glass or diamonds have low elasticity. Glass is also weak and can easily break. Therefore, it is considered brittle. In contrast, diamond is very strong and difficult to break. Thus, it is stiff. If a material is deformed and it does not return to its original shape, it is plastic. For example, both copper and aluminum can be plastically deformed. Copper is ductile, meaning that if you put a stretching force on it, it will extend to become a wire. Aluminum is malleable, meaning that if you put a compressive force on it, it will turn into a flat sheet.

III. Knowing whether a material is hard or not is important since it affects its durability. In general, hard materials last longer than soft materials. For instance, hard materials have more protection against abrasion. Abrasion is just the technical word for scratching. Therefore, the ability to resist abrasion is called scratch hardness. Also, hard materials can better resist indentation, which is when something receives compression. Therefore, the ability to resist compression is called indentation hardness.

C (CD-49)

1. The acoustical properties of a material relate to how that material responds to sound waves. This property is especially important for architectural and civil engineering. You might already know that sound absorbing-materials are used in buildings and roads.

2. Physical properties relate to the characteristics of a material that we can observe without needing a chemical reaction. Physical properties refer to things like color, density, melting or boiling temperatures, and so on. In contrast, the chemical properties of a material are observable during or after a chemical reaction.

3. Electrical properties relate to the electrical conductivity or resistivity of a material. Depending on the characteristics, we can classify materials into three categories: conductors, semiconductors, and insulators.

4. The mechanical properties of a material relate to the effect of stress that is applied to it. If we apply a force to various materials, some will elastically deform, while others will plastically deform. Typically, hard materials are more durable than soft materials.

5. Thermal properties of a material concern the effects of heat. We can think about how

a material transmits heat through thermal conductivity. In addition, we can analyze if a material expands or not when heated through thermal expansion.

GIVING A PRESENTATION

A (CD-50)

1. negative twenty-five point six-eight percent
2. three quarters
3. one point five times ten to the power of five
4. the square root of three
5. x is not equal to y
6. x is less than or equal to y
7. x is proportional to y
8. x is approximately equal to y

Unit 10 LISTENING SCRIPT

INTRODUCTION:
THINKING ABOUT FUTURE CAREERS

A (CD-51)

After the conference in Singapore, Ken is beginning to think about his future career. His original intention was to find a job at a company in Japan. However, through the experiences of meeting John, joining the short-term program in the United States, and presenting at an international conference, Ken has gradually changed his mind. He is now exploring the possibility of working abroad. Since he's already experienced Southeast Asia and the United States, Ken is considering somewhere that he has never been before, such as Europe. There, he could have many potential manufacturing companies to choose from, especially ones that produce cars and computers. However, Ken is specifically looking to intern at a company that will allow him to take advantage of his research interest. He also desires a company with international recognition. After much searching, Ken will find an interesting company called Polymer Excellence in Germany that produces green polymer products. The company seems like a perfect match for his criteria, and they are recruiting students for a chemical-engineering internship.

BACKGROUND SEARCHING: BASICS OF POLYMERS

A (CD-52)

If you compare the properties of polymers, metals, and ceramics, you will find that each has advantages and disadvantages. One of the distinctive characteristics of polymers is that they are relatively lightweight. Let's imagine that we have three coffee cups, one made of plastic, one of iron, and the other of ceramic. The plastic cup would be the lightest and, therefore, the easiest to drink. The ceramic one would be a little heavier, and you may need both hands to pick up the iron cup. Next, polymers and metals are shock-proof to a certain degree. If you accidentally dropped the cups on the floor, the plastic and iron cups would probably not break because they can resist shock. In fact, some polymers such as rubber used for vehicle tires can even absorb shock. However, the ceramic cup would most likely shatter into many pieces. Another advantage of polymers and metals is that they are easy to process; ceramics, on the other hand, are not. Now, while polymers have many advantages, there are still some downsides. First, they are weak against heat. This is why we usually cook food with metal or ceramic pots. Additionally, polymers do not have much thermal conductivity, making them even worse

for cooking. Next, polymers can deteriorate comparatively quicker, and over time, the plastic coffee cup would start to look old and ugly much faster than the other ones. While the iron cup might rust, it wouldn't degrade like the plastic one. The ceramic cup will also remain beautiful. Finally, both the polymer and ceramic cup would not conduct electricity nearly as well as the iron one.

FINDING AN INTERNSHIP TO JOIN

C (CD-53)

Our company is working to tackle three environmental issues when developing new products.

First, we endeavor to break away from our dependence on fossil fuels. Most of the currently used plastic products in the world are petroleum-based. However, petroleum, like other fossil fuels, is estimated to be depleted in the near future. We need to shift from exhaustible resources to renewable ones, and our company is taking this step forward with our bio-based products.

Second, we are engaged in reducing plastic waste. Plastic is a very versatile material, and we can find plastic products everywhere in our society today. However, its durability causes a serious problem of plastic pollution. Disposed plastic products and their debris often end up in the ocean and become harmful to marine environments. To solve this problem, we produce biodegradable plastics that can decompose into compost within a short time.

Third, we endeavor to reduce overall greenhouse gas emissions. Climate change is the biggest threat we face today. In order to prevent catastrophic consequences, we are striving to achieve net-zero carbon dioxide emissions. Even though carbon dioxide is emitted when our products are composted, this is offset when plants grow and absorb carbon dioxide. In this sense, our products can be considered carbon neutral, and we can, therefore, reduce greenhouse gas emissions.

PREPARING FOR AN INTERNSHIP

C (CD-54)

[Part one]

Ken : Hey, Lin. If you have time, could you give me a hand?

Lin : Hi, Ken! Sure, what's up?

Ken : Well, I am writing an English resume to apply for an internship in Germany. Take a look. I put my name and affiliation at the top in a bigger font size. Then I created six sections for education, research projects, technical skills, conferences and programs, skills, and languages.

Lin : It looks like a good start. OK, then let's address the left side. For education, did you also study at Osaka Tech University when you were an undergraduate?

Ken : Actually, no. I studied at the Faculty of Engineering at Naniwa Institute of Technology.

Lin : Alright, then you can put that you have a bachelor's degree in engineering from that university.

Ken : Yeah, sure. OK, let's see. Next is about my research. I would like to list my project for an autonomous fulfillment center. Oh, and also the one where I presented at an international conference entitled Engineering Applications of Material X.

Lin : That's fine. But then what can you write for your technical skills?

Ken : I was thinking about writing two things. One is analysis of technology management. The other thing I can put is failure analysis of Material X with tensile strength testing.

Lin : That'll work. Then conferences and programs. I see that you listed your participation in the international conference. Can you think of anything else?

Ken : Well, I joined a short-term program to the United States, where I studied at a university.

Lin : Oh yes, you should mention that. It should be eye-catching.

[Part two] (CD-55)

Lin : Now, let's move on to the right side of the resume. What skills do you have? Why don't you rate them on a scale from zero to five points?

Ken : Besides technical skills, what else is there?

Lin : In my opinion, you have great communication skills. You never hesitate to talk to others in the lab.

Ken : Really? Well, I do love to talk to others. OK, I came up with three items: presentations, active listening, and teamwork, all of which are important for engineers, I think.

Lin : That's smart. And if I were your supervisor, I'd give you five points for both presentations and teamwork!

Ken : Really? I'm flattered. Then I'll go ahead and mark five for both.

Lin : Any idea about other items you can add?

Ken : Hmm. I think I should add creativity. Oh, and I should also write problem-solving, as it is essential for engineers. I think I am not bad at both of them, but surely not proficient enough to put fives. I'll take one point off for each.

Lin : Lastly, how about your language skills? You are a Japanese native speaker, but I think your English is pretty good. Just write five points for each and hope that they don't test you in the interview!

Ken : No way! I am still trying to improve. Besides, they'll see my English exam score of 6.5, which is not the best. I'll just give myself three points to be safe.

Lin : Come on, Ken! Your level is higher than that!

Ken : Well, four should be fine then.

Lin : Alright. Any other languages that you can list?

Ken : I can speak a bit of German since I took a year of German language classes when I was an undergraduate.

Lin : Great! And now you're applying for an internship located in the country where you have a background in. That should give you a competitive advantage!

JOB INTERVIEW

C (CD-56)

George : Good afternoon, Mr. Nakamura. My name is George Simmel. I work in the Human Resources department at Polymer Excellence. Thank you very much for applying for our internship program.

Ken : It's nice to meet you, George. I would like to thank you for giving me this opportunity.

George : It's our pleasure. Shall we begin the interview? First of all, could you tell us a bit about yourself and your research?

Ken : Sure. I am a master's student studying engineering at Osaka Tech University and my major is Management of Technology. I chose this major because I am interested in studying technologies as well as learning how to manage them. I am currently researching how to make fulfillment centers more autonomous with robot technologies.

George : I see. And how is your research topic related to this position?

Ken : I have to admit that it's not directly related. However, I think the management of technology considers not only how to enhance efficiency and productivity, but also how to manage the impact of technology on society and the environment. While my research primarily focuses on the former, I'm also considering how to apply environmentally-friendly methods.

George : That makes sense. But there are also other companies in Japan producing green plastics like us. Why did you apply to our company, specifically?

Ken : Well, I received some international experience through a short-term program in the United States and from giving a presentation at an international conference. This experience motivated me to apply for an international internship.

George : I see. Have you thought about working abroad after graduation? Maybe here in Germany?

Ken : Well, it would be great if I could. I can even speak a little German. But to be honest, I'm not sure yet. All I can say is that I would like to work as an engineer with others worldwide to produce innovative and environmentally-friendly products.

George : Speaking of language, do you think you'll have any problems communicating with our staff members in English?

Ken : As you can see from my English examination score, my English is admittedly not perfect. However, I don't think it will be a problem. My laboratory has a variety of students from different countries, and I often talk with them in English and work as a team to conduct research together. So, I think my strength in teamwork would compensate for my lack of English skills.

George : Great. we will inform you of the results within a couple weeks. Thank you for coming.

Ken : Thank you, George, for your time.

Unit 1 **ANSWERS**

INTRODUCTION: LET'S MEET KEN

A

1. Japan
2. Management of Technology
3. Traveling
4. Meet an exchange student

B

1. Are you familiar with
2. hopes to
3. By the way
4. looking forward to
5. show him around

C

1. modifications   2. incorporate
3. rough draft   4. sketches
5. prototype

D

2, 4, 6, 8

EMAIL EXCHANGE

A

1. Allow me to give some
2. I was wondering if we
3. I'd be happy to meet you
4. I look forward to seeing you

B

Sample Answers:

Dear John,

1. It's nice to meet you. Please call me Ken. It's no problem with you messaging me directly. Actually, I was thinking about getting in contact with you before you

emailed me. By the way, don't worry about not knowing Japanese. Most of our lab mates know English, so it shouldn't be a problem.

2. Allow me to give you some information about myself too. I am currently a first-year master's student majoring in Management of Technology. I'm very active and really enjoy traveling. I've traveled to Guam when I was young. But other than that, I haven't been abroad.

3. Regarding your question, yes, I'd be happy to meet you anytime. Please contact me once you've arrived in Japan, and we can figure out a time. And how about we meet on campus at building A1?

4. I'm happy to help with anything you need, and I look forward to meeting you.

C

1. c   2. a   3. a   4. a

MEETING THE EXCHANGE STUDENT

A

1st e $\Rightarrow$ 2nd d $\Rightarrow$ 3rd c $\Rightarrow$ 4th b $\Rightarrow$ 5th a

B

1. I was wondering if you could help me. I'm trying to figure out where Building A1 is.
2. I volunteered to help you out, so let me know if there's anything you need.
3. I'd like to show you around campus if that's OK with you.
4. Would you be interested in participating in a competition?

KEN'S RESEARCH

A

1. technical   2. considered
3. constraints   4. incorporation

B

1. b   2. c

C

2nd c ⇒ 3rd d ⇒ 4th b ⇒ 5th f ⇒ 6th e

DESIGN CONCEPT

A

1. d   2. c   3. b   4. a   5. f

B

1. b   2. b   3. a   4. b

C

1. They are large and heavy and require a place to park.
2. They propose a lightweight and portable bike for people who need fast and convenient transportation (but do not have access to bicycle parking lots or do not want to carry a heavy bike).
3. c
4. a

Unit 2 ANSWERS

INTRODUCTION: WORKING IN A LAB

A

1. loads   2. Nevertheless
3. ensure   4. conduct
5. sufficient

B

1. deformable   2. fluid   3. rigid

C

1. rigid   2. fluid   3. deformable

D

1. bear a load   2. static
3. dynamic   4. velocity
5. acceleration   6. friction
7. rigid

E

1. support beam   2. is
3. isn't   4. don't
5. rocket   6. is
7. is   8. do

SAFETY PROCEDURES IN THE LAB

A

1. e   2. d   3. b   4. c   5. a
6. g   7. h   8. j   9. f   10. i

B

1. √   2. ✕   3. √   4. √   5. ✕
6. ✕

C

1. a   2. b   3. a   4. b

D

1. ✕   2. ✕   3. O
4. ✕   5. (blank) 6. ✕

LEARNING ABOUT STATIC PRINCIPLES

A

1. c   2. b   3. c

B

1. e   2. g   3. h   4. f
5. b   6. c   7. d

C

1. b   2. e   3. c   4. d   5. a

LEARNING ABOUT DYNAMIC PRINCIPLES

A

1. accelerate
2. velocity
3. decelerate
4. pivot

B

1. accelerate
2. decelerate
3. top velocity
4. pivot

C

Sample Answers:

1. The manned helicopter can carry a higher load.
2. The drone can start and stop moving faster because it has higher acceleration and deceleration.
3. A drone can be used for aerial photography because it is a cheaper alternative.
4. A helicopter can be used to rescue people because its carrying capacity is high.

A WELCOME DINNER FOR THE NEW LAB MEMBERS

A

1. c   2. b   3. a   4. b   5. a

B

1. d-a-c-b
2. d-a-c-b
3. b-a-c-d
4. b-d-c-a

C

1. c   2. a   3. a   4. a   5. b

Unit 3 ANSWERS

INTRODUCTION: APPLYING FOR A STUDY ABROAD PROGRAM

A

1. b   2. c   3. b   4. a

ARRIVING AT HIS DESTINATION: TALKING WITH HIS HOST FAMILY

A

1. c   2. a   3. a   4. b   5. b

ATTENDING A SEMINAR: BASICS OF ELECTRICITY

A

1. electromotive force
2. electrical resistance
3. electrical charge
4. siemens
5. farad
6. henry
7. magnetic flux
8. magnetic flux density

B

1. circuits
2. Direct
3. voltage
4. transformer
5. Alternating
6. utilized
7. transmit

C

1. direct
2. alternating

D

1. d   2. b   3. c   4. a

ATTENDING A SEMINAR: THE WORLD-FAMOUS INVENTOR

A

1. d   2. f   3. b
4. e   5. a   6. c

B

1. False   2. False   3. False   4. True

D

1. I find out what the world needs. Then I go ahead and invent it.
2. I have not failed. I've just found 10,000 ways that won't work.
3. Many of life's failures are people who did not realize how close they were to success when they gave up.
4. Just because something doesn't do what you planned it to do doesn't mean it's useless.

WATCHING THE NEWS ABOUT ELECTRIC CARS

A

1. c   2. a   3. a   4. c   5. c

B

1. d   2. a

C

1. It depends on   2. speaking of
3. here and there   4. pros and cons
5. Let's see

E

Sample Answers:
Pros
It can be more environmentally-friendly.
It can be cheaper to drive long distances since it has better fuel efficiency.
Acceleration is smoother.
Electric cars are quieter.

Cons
The distance that you can drive on a single charge is limited.
The price of electric cars is relatively higher.
The amount of nearby electric charging stations is usually fewer than that of gas stations.
It takes more time to charge the batteries.

Unit 4 ANSWERS

INTRODUCTION: SENDING AN EMAIL TO A PROFESSOR

A

1. The name of the laboratory is the Future Energy Lab.
2. A few months ago, Ken saw Professor Brown giving a presentation on TV.
3. Professor Brown emphasizes not just doing research but also cooperating with companies to benefit society.
4. Ken wants to visit the laboratory in mid-August, if possible.

B

1. a   2. b   3. b   4. b

C

1. a   2. a   3. b

D

1. (Would you mind telling me) how much the program costs?
2. (Please let me know) if I need to take the examination.
3. (Could I know) your availability? Or: (Could I know) what your availability is?

4. (Could you tell me) how many students are in your lab?

5. (Do you know) where the professor's office is?

6. (Would you kindly tell me) which textbook we will use?

PREPARATION FOR THE LAB VISIT: ENERGY AND TEMPERATURE

A

1. Mechanical	2. Electrical
3. Thermal	4. Radiant
5. Chemical	6. Nuclear
7. Gravitational	8. Elastic

B

1. Kinetic   2. Potential

PREPARATION FOR THE LAB VISIT: KINETIC ENERGY

A

1. e   2. c   3. a   4. d
5. f   6. g   7. h   8. b

B

1. consist	2. transmission
3. generating	4. transforms
5. method	6. generated
7. referred	

C

1. a   2. c   3. d   4. b   5. e

D

1. Convection
2. Conduction
3. Radiation

E

1. c   2. b   3. c   4. a

F

1. False   2. False   3. True   4. True

VISITING PROFESSOR BROWN'S LAB: MEETING A STUDENT

A

1. a   2. b   3. a   4. c   5. b

C

1. a   2. c   3. a   4. b   5. a

D

1st a ⇒ 2nd c ⇒ 3rd d ⇒ 4th b

DISCUSSION: RENEWABLE ENERGY

A

1. according to recent news
2. If I am not mistaken
3. As I was mentioning before
4. That's exactly what I was going to say
5. I agree with you on that point

B

1. It may soon play an important role as a solution for storing renewable energy.
2. It's difficult to store the collected power when a lot is produced.
3. Chris's concern is that it will cost a lot of money and it's important to know who will pay for it.

Unit 5 ANSWERS

INTRODUCTION: ATTENDING A WORKSHOP

A
1. c   2. a   3. a   4. b

B
Sample Answers:
1. I happened to meet an old classmate at a workshop about future technology.
2. Given the importance of clean energy, the government focused on nuclear power plants.
3. Please make sure to fill out the application prior to attending the workshop.

D
1. d   2. g   3. c
4. b   5. f   6. a

E
1. a   2. a   3. a   4. b   5. b

PREPARING FOR THE WORKSHOP

A
1. counting   2. finding
3. securing   4. storing
5. communicating   6. calculating
7. sorting   8. processing

B
1. Hardware represents the physical body of a machine.
2. Software represents the brain of a machine.
3. They are interdependent. Software gives commands to hardware regarding tasks that need to be performed.

4. A firewall monitors and protects ingoing and outgoing internet activity.

C
software: 4, 6, 7
hardware: 1, 2, 3, 5

D
1. False   2. False   3. True   4. False
5. False   6. False   7. False   8. True

E
1. !   2. #   3.   -
4. *   5. ,   6.   @
7. /   8. "   "   9.   (   )

F
1. c   2. b   3. a   4. c   5. b
6. a   7. d   8. b   9. a   10. d
11. c   12. b   13. a   14. d   15. c

DISCUSSION: ARTIFICIAL INTELLIGENCE PREDICTIONS

A
Sample Answers:
1. AI uses advanced algorithms that copy the behavior of a human brain.
2. Having a laptop with AI would be beneficial because it can carry out many useful tasks independently.
3. AI can allow us to save time by assisting us with tasks that we do not want to do. We will have more time and freedom.
4. If true AI can be achieved, it may be dangerous to humans because machines will take over their jobs.

B
1. diminish   2. justified
3. exceeded   4. precise
5. implications

C

1. 40   2. 73

D

1. 55   2. 13   3. 32

E

1. 99   2. 89   3. Software engineer

PRESENTATION: ARTIFICIAL INTELLIGENCE PREDICTIONS

A

1. I appreciate this opportunity to present my research
2. I am going to give a presentation regarding the topic of
3. let me begin by outlining
4. I will begin by providing background information on
5. I will introduce two opposite opinions
6. I will describe how
7. let me summarize my
8. I would like to emphasize that

B

1. False   2. True   3. True   4. False

Unit 6 ANSWERS

INTRODUCTION: THE BACKGROUND OF A COMPETITION

A

1. a number of   2. aspects
3. relevant   4. encounter
5. pay attention   6. find out

B

1. a   2. b   3. a
4. c   5. c   6. a

C

1. come up with   2. pay attention
3. a number of   4. encountered
5. relevant

AN ADVERTISEMENT FOR AN ENGINEERING COMPETITION

A

1. b   2. b   3. a   4. c   5. c

B

1. The event will be held at Lake Biwa on November 2nd from 7:00 – 16:00.
2. The contestants will be judged on three aspects: airtime, flight distance, and the creativity of design.
3. Yes, the event is free for spectators.
4. Team members must demonstrate their ability to swim, be in good physical condition, and pay the entry fee.
5. People can find more information from the event's website under "Event Rules and Safety".

C

Sample Answers:

1. They are talking about competing in an event.
2. They can receive a scholarship if they win. They can also receive extra credit for participating.
3. The group sounds like they are interested, so it appears that they will participate.
4. Lin needs to check her schedule first before she can decide.
5. This event sounds interesting because it seems like a great opportunity to make new friends and have fun.

D

1. c   2. b   3. d   4. a

DOING THE MEASUREMENTS I: DRAWING UP THE BLUEPRINTS

A

a. multimeter   b. stopwatch
c. scale   d. tape measure
e. thermometer

1. b   2. a   3. c   4. d   5. e

B

1. overall height   2. wingspan
3. overall length   4. fuselage width

C

1. circumference   2. diameter
3. radius   4. arc

D

1. d   2. b   3. c   4. f   5. e

WORKING TOGETHER TO PLAN THE PROJECT

A

1. Paragraph 2   2. Paragraph 4
3. Paragraph 1   4. Paragraph 3

B

1. True   2. False   3. False   4. False

C

1. ✗
2. ○, September 15th
3. ○, October 1st
4. ✗
5. ○, October 15th
6. ○, November 1st

DOING THE MEASUREMENTS II: ACCURACY

A

1. c   2. a   3. b
4. f   5. d   6. e

B

1. ○   2. ○   3. ✗
4. ○   5. ✗   6. ✗

LEARNING ABOUT MECHANISMS

A

1. a   2. b   3. b

B

1. a   2. c   3. b

COMPETING IN THE EVENT

A

1. c   2. c   3. a   4. b   5. a

B

b

Unit 7 **ANSWERS**

INTRODUCTION: TAKING A CLASS

A

1. b   2. c   3. a   4. c

B

1. False   2. False   3. True

4. True   5. False

C

1. put the theories into practice
2. for this purpose   3. in charge of

PREPARING FOR THE TOUR: SAFETY TIPS

A

1. ○   2. ✗   3. ○   4. ✗
5. ○   6. ○   7. ✗   8. ✗

B

1. They might get injured by sharp corners or jagged surfaces if they expose their skin in the shipyard.
2. Students are instructed to wear sneakers because they are comfortable and protect their feet.
3. Yes, it is. But you must receive permission first.

C

Sample Answers:
1. You are not supposed to eat or drink in the laboratory as you may contaminate the results of an experiment.
2. You are obligated to wear eye protection when welding due to the intense light and high temperature.
3. Employees are not permitted to enter the facility without wearing a hard hat because heavy objects might fall and crush one's head.
4. Students are required to put their smartphones away during exams in order to prevent cheating.

UNDERSTANDING FLUID AND AIR DYNAMICS

A

1. e   2. d   3. c   4. b   5. a

B

1. lift   2. drag
3. thrust   4. weight
5. buoyancy   6. drag
7. thrust   8. weight

C

1.
(a) hull   (b) strut
(c) hydrofoil   (d) teardrop
(e) airflow   (f) lift
2.
(a) True   (b) False
(c) True   (d) True

D

1. b   2. d   3. a   4. c   5. e

THE CLASS TOURS A SHIPYARD

A

1. Lofting   2. Bending
3. Assembling blocks 4. Painting
5. Launching

B

9-7-4-5-6-8-2-3

C

1. NCC is an automatic system to cut parts of a ship from steel slabs.
2. Since automated machines cannot bend parts like skilled crafts(wo)men, craftsmanship is needed to create the curvy shapes of a ship.
3. It is a method whereby a ship is divided into several blocks and assembled separately.

LEARNING ABOUT CORPORATE SOCIAL RESPONSIBILITY (CSR)

A

1. c   2. b   3. d   4. c   5. a

B

1. b   2. a   3. c

C

1. c   2. b   3. a

FOLLOWING A GOVERNMENT-INITIATED PROJECT: i-Shipping

A

1. The project aims to revitalize the Japanese marine industries to be cost-competitive in the world markets, produce high-quality products, and deliver high-quality service.
2. In order to return to the top in the global market, Japan needs to take advantage of its strength in productivity while overcoming its weakness in cost competitiveness.
3. The key is the transformation of conventional shipyards into smart ones with the help of IoT, big data, and AI.

B

1. simulate   2. valid
3. transparency   4. investment
5. anticipate   6. optimization

INTRODUCTION: PARTICIPATING IN A SPECIAL PROGRAM

B

1. as usual   2. You must be
3. found out   4. take part
5. You know what   6. up for it

C

1. b-d-c-a   2. a-d-c-b
3. a-c-d-b   4. d-a-c-b

ATTENDING A LECTURE: BASICS OF MACHINING

A

1. d   2. a   3. b   4. c   5. e
6. h   7. i   8. f   9. j   10. g

B

1. Machining
2. chips
3. coolant
4. Computer Numerical Control
5. Computer-Aided Manufacturing

C

1. The main factors to consider are the properties of the materials and the required edge quality.
2. We will need to consider the material's ability to bear the mechanical stress.
3. We will need to address heat-affected zones/heat distortion.
4. It is the extra work needed to finish materials after they are machined.

D

1. Guillotining
2. Flame cutting
3. Electric discharge machining (EDM)
4. Plasma cutting
5. Ultra high-pressure water jet cutting

LEARNING JOINING TECHNIQUES AT A COMPANY

A

1. Non-mechanical   2. Permanent
3. screws   4. rivets
5. welding   6. adhesives
(5 and 6 are in no particular order)

B

1. c   2. c   3. a
4. mortise: c, tenon: d,
   gap: b, wedge: a

C

1. Vibrations   2. shock
(1 and 2 are in no particular order)
3. play   4. wedge
5. transverse

UNDERSTANDING THE BACKGROUND: SMART MANUFACTURING

A

1. put   2. integrated
3. perceived   4. encompasses
5. enable

B

1. True   2. True   3. True
4. False   5. False

C

1. a   2. d   3. c   4. b   5. b

VISITING A STEEL COMPANY

A

1. b   2. a   3. e   4. c   5. d

B

1. It is difficult for machines to decide how to weld components with unique shapes.
2. There is little space to work during block assembling.
3. IoT collects data on welding machines or issues to increase productivity.

WORKING ON A PROJECT AT THE COMPANY

A

1. think it over: to consider something before accepting it
2. follow through on: when someone completes their responsibility or task
3. going well: when something has good results and progress is moving forward

B

1. The deadline is getting near. We have to make sure that we can follow through on the project.
2. I don't need an answer today. Please think it over and let me know sometime this week.
3. It appears that the work is going well. You're all doing an excellent job.
4. I know you feel like you can't take on more responsibilities at this time. However, I really need your help.

C

1. a   2. b   3. b   4. c

D

1. b   2. c   3. a   4. c

INTRODUCTION: RECEIVING AN EMAIL FROM JOHN

A

2nd e $\Rightarrow$ 3rd c $\Rightarrow$ 4th b $\Rightarrow$ 5th d

B

1. c   2. b   3. c   4. a   5. b

BACKGROUND SEARCHING: FINDING A CONFERENCE TO ATTEND

A

1. d   2. a   3. d

C

1. True   2. False   3. True   4. False

SIGNING UP FOR A CONFERENCE

A

1. Even though Material X is an important material in the industry, its mechanical properties are not well investigated yet.
2. The purpose is to examine a way to increase the limit of the load capacity of Material X.
3. Material X is very fragile and sensitive to mechanical and thermal loading conditions.

B

1. Ken Nakamura
2. Graduate School of Engineering, Osaka Tech University
3. 86-6879-555

4. knakamura@ot.ac.jp
5. student poster presentation

C

2nd e $\Rightarrow$ 3rd d $\Rightarrow$ 4th c $\Rightarrow$ 5th b

D

1. c-b-a-d   2. d-c-b-a
3. c-b-d-a   4. b-a-c-d
5. a-b-d-c

PREPARING FOR A POSTER PRESENTATION

A

1. Sodium is an element.
2. Salt is a compound; it is composed of sodium and chlorine.
3. Brine is a mixture; it is comprised of water and salt.
4. Bronze is an alloy; it is made up of tin and copper.

(underlined parts are in no particular order)

B

1. tension   2. compression
3. tensile   4. elongate
5. compressive   6. tensile
7. compressive   8. elastic
9. brittle   10. stiff
11. plastic   12. ductile
13. malleable   14. durability
15. hard   16. soft
17. scratch   18. indentation

C

1. D, b   2. B, a   3. C, d
4. E, e   5. A, c

GIVING A PRESENTATION

A

1. h   2. e   3. a   4. c

5. d   6. b   7. g   8. f

B

1. d   2. c   3. f   4. b   5. e

WATCHING A PLENARY

A

1. f   2. b   3. g   4. h
5. e   6. a   7. c   8. d

B

1. Straw can compensate for the weakness of mud bricks, which have low tensile strength, and thus can reinforce the bricks.
2. Bricks have a mud matrix reinforced with straw, just like fiberglass has a plastic matrix reinforced with glass fibers.
3. Fiberglass is used in various products such as ship hulls, airfoils, auto bodies, traffic lights, water pipes, and more.
4. The C-glass fiber has high chemical resistance and, therefore, is suitable for corrosive acid environments.
5. The S-glass fiber has the highest percentage of elongation and, therefore, can extend the most.
6. The A-glass fiber has the highest value of the thermal expansion coefficient and thus changes the most when heated.

INTRODUCTION:
THINKING ABOUT FUTURE CAREERS

A

1. a   2. d   3. b   4. c

B

1. a   2. c   3. b   4. g
5. e   6. d   7. f

C

1. Lin is considering either working at a university as a researcher or working for a company.
2. She is not sure if she can handle the work required to get a job, all while attending classes and conducting her research.
3. While Japanese students start job hunting when they are in universities, students in Lin's country begin to work as interns after graduation.

BACKGROUND SEARCHING:
BASICS OF POLYMERS

A

1. −   2. +   3. −   4. +
5. −   6. +   7. −

C

1. molecules   2. atoms
3. natural   4. synthetic
5. melt   6. set
7. transparent   8. cure
9. permanently   10. elastic

FINDING AN INTERNSHIP TO JOIN

A

1. derived   2. finite
3. substitutes   4. consume
5. neutral

B

1. b   2. d   3. c   4. a

C

1. dependence   2. exhaustible
3. durability   4. compost
5. net   6. offset

PREPARING FOR AN INTERNSHIP

A

1. False   2. False
3. True   4. True
5. False (both must agree)
6. True

B

	Similar word	Opposite word
1.	identical	different
2.	inhabit	leave
3.	reciprocal	independent
4.	compensate	deprive
5.	infer	disbelieve

C

1. engineering
2. Autonomous
3. Failure analysis
4. Short-term
5. ■ ■ ■ ■ ■
6. Teamwork
7. ■ ■ ■ ■ □
8. ■ ■ ■ ■ □
9. (Score: 6.5)

JOB INTERVIEW

A

1. f   2. b   3. a
4. e   5. d   6. c

C

1. a, b   2. b, c   3. a, c   4. a, b

KEYWORDS

Unit 1 Designing and Modeling

Academic Vocabulary	Technical Vocabulary	Useful Expressions
analyze approach benefit complement concept consider constraint distribute formula incorporate significance	access design consideration improvement model modification proposal prototype rough draft sketch technical	**General** by the way (be) familiar with … figure out … help (you) out I'd be happy to I hope to (see you again) I was wondering if … show (you) around would you be interested in …? **Thematic: Introductions** allow me to introduce (myself) Hi, I'm (Ken). And you are? It's nice to meet you I look forward to …

Unit 2 Static and Dynamic Principles

Academic Vocabulary	Technical Vocabulary	Useful Expressions
approximate circumstance conclude conduct ensure establish hence nevertheless prohibit sufficient	accelerate bear a load compression decelerate equilibrium friction pivot rigid/deformable/fluid (body) shearing static/dynamic (force) stress tension torque velocity	**General** feel free to … stop by that's about it you can reach me (at/on) … **Thematic: Instructions I** go over (the plans) in principle keep in mind that … make sure to …

Unit 3 Electricity

Academic Vocabulary	Technical Vocabulary	Useful Expressions
acquire	alternating/direct	**General**
allocate	(current)	don't mention it
driving force	circuit	go ahead (and try)
innovation	coulomb	help yourself
investigate	farad	here and there
patent	henry	it depends on …
primary	inventor	let's see
pursue	ohm	make yourself at home
utilize	siemens	pros and cons
	tesla	speaking of …
	transformer	wish me luck
	transmit	
	volt	**Thematic: Stating opinions**
	voltage	from what I know ….
	weber	I agree with you
		I believe …
		I doubt it
		I know what you mean
		in my opinion ….

Unit 4 Energy and Temperature

Academic Vocabulary	Technical Vocabulary	Useful Expressions
consist	conduction	**General**
contribute	convection	in charge of …
convert	fossil fuels	I would like to …
generate	generator	let's get started
implement	geothermal power	no way
initial	hydroelectric power	take it easy
method	petroleum	that sounds good
pose	radiant/gravitational/	
refer	kinetic (energy)	**Thematic: Discussions**
regulate	radiation	according to …
transform	(nuclear) reactor	as I (mentioned) before
	turbine	If I am not mistaken
		(I agree with you) on that point
		that's exactly what I was going to say

Unit 5 Computing and Future Technology

Academic Vocabulary	Technical Vocabulary	Useful Expressions
confirm	artificial intelligence	**General**
consent	asterisk	given (the importance of ....)
diminish	'at' sign	(I) happen to (know)
exceed	database	subject to ...
exclude	exclamation mark	
implication	firewall	**Thematic: Presentations I**
indicate	hash	I appreciate this opportunity
justify	hyphen	I am going to give a presentation
precise	operating system	regarding ...
provide	parentheses	let me begin by ...
specify	quotation mark	then I will introduce ...
vary		finally, I will describe ...
		I would like to emphasize that ...
		let me summarize ...

Unit 6 Measurements and Mechanisms

Academic Vocabulary	Technical Vocabulary	Useful Expressions
adequate	accurate	**General**
aspect	arc *shape	a number of ...
convene	assembly	at all times
criteria	circumference	comply with ...
demonstrate	clearance	pay attention
differentiate	component	(we) shouldn't have ...
encounter	cross section	
inadequate	diameter	**Thematic: Working together I**
relevant	dimension	come up with (a plan)
	fuselage	cut corners
	mechanism	draw up (blueprints)
	permissible	follow up (on/with) ...
	radius	give (me) a hand
	tolerance	it turns out that ...
		miss the mark
		work out (fine)

Unit 7 Fluid and Air Dynamics		
Academic Vocabulary	Technical Vocabulary	Useful Expressions
anticipate	airflow	**General**
endeavor	assemble	for this purpose
engage	buoyancy	put (a theory) into practice
incline	crest	
investment	drag	**Thematic: Instructions II**
optimization	hull	(be) allowed to ...
restore	hydrofoil/airfoil	(be) obligated to ...
retain	install	(be) permitted to ...
simulate	join (pieces together)	(be) required to ...
transparency	launch	(be) supposed to ...
valid	lift	due to ...
	lofting	in order to ...
	profile	so as (not) to ...
	propel	
	strut	
	teardrop	
	thrust	
	trough	

Unit 8 Manufacturing, Assembly, and Components		
Academic Vocabulary	Technical Vocabulary	Useful Expressions
accumulate	adhesive	**General**
compile	aid	as usual
enable	arc *electricity	to put it simply
encompass	chip (swarf)	(I'm) up for (it)
integrate	coolant	You know what?
interact	discharge	you must be (Ken)
isolate	distortion	
perceive	erosion	**Thematic: Working together II**
refine	machine (a workpiece)	count on (me)
	mortise	follow through (on/with) ...
	net (result)	go well
	nut and bolt	hold off on (doing it)
	rivet	take on (extra work)
	screw	think (it) over
	tenon	touch base with (you)
	torch	
	wedge	
	welding	

Unit 9 Materials Science

Academic Vocabulary	Technical Vocabulary	Useful Expressions
compensate	brittle	**General**
constituent	compound	do (me) a favor
discrete	compressive	(be) expected to …
distinctive	ductile	get by
dominate	durable	in what follows
inhibit	elastic	inform (you) of …
reinforce	element	make a change to …
versatile	elongate	run into …
	malleable	send (my) regards to …
	plastic	take into account
	proportional	time flies
	scratch/indentation	
	(hardness)	**Thematic: Presentations II**
	stiff	… is/are not well investigated yet
	tensile	the results indicate …
		this research proposes a new
		method for …

Unit 10 Biotechnology and Applied Chemistry

Academic Vocabulary	Technical Vocabulary	Useful Expressions
assume	atom	**General**
consume	combustion	bear in mind
dependence	compost	come in handy
derive	cure	cross (my) mind
equivalent	decomposition	hand in (paperwork)
exhaustible	deterioration	keep an eye on …
finite	fermentation	make up (my) mind
mutual	molecule	slip (my) mind
neutral	opaque	
offset	permanently	**Thematic: Job interviews**
reimburse	photosynthesis	I don't think it will be a problem
reside	set	(this experience) motivated (me)
substitute	shock/heat-proof	to …
	soften	my strength (in …) would
	synthetic	compensate for my lack of …
	temporarily	to be honest, I am not sure yet

date _____

Name _____ Student ID _____

_____

_____

_____

_____

_____

_____

_____

_____

_____

_____

_____

_____

_____

_____

_____

_____

_____

_____

_____

_____

_____

_____

_____

_____

_____

_____

Acknowledgments

This textbook would not have been possible without the support of our colleagues, students, and family members. We would first like to sincerely thank both Kiyoshi Fujita, the director of the Center for International Affairs within the Graduate School of Engineering at Osaka University, and Seiko Kaneko, who currently works at the JICA Research Institute, for entrusting us with the task of creating this textbook and offering advice. Next, we would like to thank Ian Allensworth, Charles Clark, Ellen Yoshioka, and the many students who participated for their editing support and feedback. We also wish to thank Kai Shimada, Callum Fisher, and Rachel Brindley for their voice acting. We appreciate Hardlock Industry Co., Ltd. for kindly allowing us to mention their product. We thank Osaka University Press, especially Sachiko Kurihara, for patiently supporting us until the end. Finally, we wish to thank our families for allowing us to take the time to finish this work. We dedicate this textbook to the engineering students who are eager to improve their English to lead global careers. We hope that this textbook will help you become confident in your English proficiency to share and present your important ideas to people around the world.

本教科書は、多くの同僚、学生、家族の支えがなければ到底完成し得ませんでした。新たな教科書の作成の機会を下さり、有益な助言を頂きました、大阪大学大学院工学研究科国際交流推進センターの藤田清士センター長、金子聖子先生（現 JICA 研究所）に心より感謝申し上げます。同様に、本教科書作成段階で草稿を何度も読み、問題を実際に解き、貴重なコメントをくださった Charles Clark さん、Ian Allensworth さん、Ellen Yoshioka さん、工学研究科の学生さん、リスニング教材の録音にご協力いただいた嶋田開さん、Callum Fisher さん、Rachel Brindley さんにここに謝意を示します。また、HLN ハードロックナットを紹介させて頂く許可を頂きましたハードロック工業株式会社様に厚く御礼申し上げます。この教科書の出版にご尽力いただいた大阪大学出版会の皆さま、特にご担当頂いた栗原佐智子さんは辛抱強く、粘り強く私たちを支えて下さり、本教科書の完成にご尽力頂きました。ご献身に深く感謝いたします。最後に、この教科書作成にあたって支えてくれた家族に感謝します。本教科書を英語力を磨き世界で活躍したいと願っている工学を専攻する学生に捧げます。この教科書を通して彼／彼女たちが自身の英語力に自信を持ち、その素晴らしい考えを世界中の人々に伝える助けになれば幸いです。

Shawn Andersson, Maho Nakahashi, Ryogo Yanagida
Osaka, March 2020

About the authors

Shawn Andersson　アンダーソン　ショーン

Specially Appointed Assistant Professor, Center for International Affairs, Graduate School of Engineering, Osaka University

TESOL Certificate, Columbia University

M.B.A. in International Project Management, Kyoto University

Research Field: Applied Linguistics

大阪大学大学院工学研究科国際交流推進センター特任助教（常勤）

京都大学経営管理大学院博士前期課程修了

コロンビア大学 TESOL Certificate

専門分野：英語教育

Maho Nakahashi　中橋　真穂

Assistant Professor, Center for International Affairs, Graduate School of Engineering, Osaka University

Ph.D. in Language and Culture, Graduate School of Language and Culture, Osaka University

Research Field: Cross Cultural Studies, Ethnicity

大阪大学大学院工学研究科国際交流推進センター助教

大阪大学大学院言語文化研究科言語文化学専攻博士後期課程修了

専門分野：異文化理解教育、エスニシティ

Ryogo Yanagida　柳田　亮吾

Specially Appointed Assistant Professor, Center for Multilingual Education, Osaka University

Ph.D. in Language and Culture, Graduate School of Language and Culture, Osaka University

Research Field: Sociolinguistics (im/politeness studies), Critical Discourse Studies

大阪大学マルチリンガル教育センター特任助教（常勤）

大阪大学大学院言語文化研究科言語文化学専攻博士後期課程修了

専門分野：社会言語学（イン／ポライトネス研究）・批判的談話研究

Let's Learn! Engineering English for Practical Applications

発行日　2020年4月13日　初版第1刷　　　　〔検印廃止〕

編著者　Shawn Andersson
　　　　Maho Nakahashi
　　　　Ryogo Yanagida

発行所　大阪大学出版会
　　　　代表者　三成賢次
　　　　〒565-0871
　　　　大阪府吹田市山田丘2-7　大阪大学ウエストフロント
　　　　電話：06-6877-1614（代表）　FAX：06-6877-1617
　　　　URL　http://www.osaka-up.or.jp

イラスト　　　　　中橋真穂
カバーデザイン　　LEMONed 大前靖寿
印刷・製本　　　　株式会社 遊文舎